What to Do with the Kids on a Rainy Day . . .

What to Do with the Kids on a Rainy Day . . .

or in a car,
or on a plane,
or when they're sick . . .

Adrienne Katz

St. Martin's Press
New York

Acknowledgments

Thanks to the many children and parents who gave me their suggestions, ideas and advice: Karen Gooding for help with the musical ideas, Liane for being a great companion on rainy days, and the children at Prior Weston School who collected rhymes and games. Steve Gonski for help and advice. The Lewer family for Phantôme and Egyptian Mummies, and my family for patience and support.

Designed by Zena Flax
Illustrations by Cetra Long and Zena Flax

Library of Congress Cataloging-in-Publication Data

Katz, Adrienne.
      What to do with the kids on a rainy day—: or in a car, or on a plane, or when they're sick— /Adrienne Katz.
                  p.   cm.
          ISBN 0-312-03451-2
            1. Creative activities and seat work.
    2. Amusements. I. Title.
      GV1203.K345   1989
      649'.51—dc20   89-10315
                                                      CIP

First published in Great Britain by Judy Piatkus (Publishers) Limited, under the title *Have Fun with Cooped-Up Kids*.

10 9 8 7 6 5 4 3

contents

In memory of Dad who always said, "Be resourceful!"

on imagination

Apart from years of parenting, learning from kids, and writing books with children in mind, there were a few distinct triggers behind my decision to write this book. The coldest winter in forty years had something to do with it! We were certainly indoors most of the time for many months. Then, there was the impact of a couple of statements I read within a few days of each other.

The first was from a civilian passenger who had been held hostage in an airline hijack. He expressed what many prisoners have said before him. "I'd never have survived without my powers of imagination. Each day I remembered an experience I'd had, and relived it in my mind's eye. That is how I remained sane."

I was struck by the power of the human mind to escape reality and physical limits with its ability to imagine and to hold on to dreams. Hopefully we won't find ourselves in such an extreme situation as this hostage, but our imaginations and those of our children can expand horizons whenever necessary. There are periods of ill health, worry, loneliness, restricted movement, boredom, lack of space, friends, funds or family which we have to get through. Indeed, kids often feel that they are held hostage by an adult world.

This powerful tool should be developed rather than subdued. Through it we would be giving our children a special power for survival and pleasure. Sharpen powers of observation, and life is infinitely more fascinating. Encourage a child's creativity and you open doors into other worlds of inspiration and invention.

A couple of days later I came across this quotation. Einstein said, "The gift of fantasy has meant more to me than my talent for absorbing positive knowledge." If confirmation were needed, this was it. I set about exploring this idea with children who gave me their enthusiastic support and help.

Adults may well ask, "Of course, if children have this rich imagination and power of observation to start with, why should we need to enhance it?" I wish this question did not need asking, but there are so many ways in which modern living and education serve to subdue or blunt this side of the mind as the child grows older, that we are in danger of losing it.

If fantasy in Einstein's remark means having the faith to try something, to experiment and seek solutions when none seems apparent or possible, then we also need to create an atmosphere in which a child can experiment and maybe fail. Most of us adults need encouragement to be understanding and respectful of the child's effort in an impatient world, to use our imagination to understand what the endeavor of the moment might mean to a particular child. I offer as comfort to the parent of an inquisitive, tireless little experimenter, Maria Montessori's words. . . . "The unknown energy that can help humanity is that which lies hidden in the child."

This book is a collection of suggestions to trigger your imagination and that of your children. A key to inner doors leading to shared fun and escape from tedium.

Adrienne Katz

words of advice

This is not a 'What shall we do?' book for parents to use to send kids off with. It is, I hope, a sharing book for family fun, a source book to dip into and return to. Many of the games and ideas have been suggested by children, and all of them have been tested and enjoyed.

I have included suggestions which will trigger the imagination and be fun to do at any time. They have been especially chosen to be handy when you're in a tight spot, wondering what to do with your restless 'cooped-up kids'. The right game at the right time can save a long car journey from descending into a hellish experience. A good laugh can help to pass the long hours of sickness and convalescence. A flight into fantasy will expand your child's horizons far beyond the walls of a small room. Stimulating activities can be a lifeline for both parent and child.

In this book I have made suggestions which will appeal to a wide age range. There are those the child can do alone, and others for two or more to tackle. Parents' participation will usually increase the pleasure but is seldom essential.

In the chapters on **Games without toys** and **Travelling**, there is an emphasis on ideas that don't involve toys. When you are rushed and busy, the last thing you want to have to carry about, look after, gather up and share out is play equipment! These games use fingers, paper and pencil, mental agility or wordplay, to name a few 'portable diversions'. Many of them are traditional and have been handed down over the years. You'll probably know quite a number of them and I hope will enjoy playing them with another generation.

Cooking and **gardening** are fulfilling pastimes; cooking rather more filling than any other!

They offer children a chance to learn useful skills while having fun.

The chapters on **In a creative mood**, **Fun and fantasy** and **Sound and rhythm** contain ideas for indoors; rainy days, confined spaces, thin walls, limited materials and much imagination. They offer an escape through dressing up, magic, story-telling, music, painting and other art techniques, and will provide hours of satisfying creative play and shared adventure.

Games for groups will help to break the ice when children are thrown together or a group needs some structured games for a while.

The final chapter on what to do to keep a **sick child** happily absorbed will come in useful in all families from time to time. The ideas in **What to Do With the Kids on a Rainy Day** have been grouped in chapters for easy reference, but many of them are interchangeable so don't hesitate to mix them up and use travel games for a sick child if that's what works for you.

The play experience

Although this book suggests ideas for keeping children (and adults) happy and absorbed, I hope it doesn't give an impression of 'organised play'. Such play forms only part of the play experience and is hopefully counterpointed by periods of un-supervised creative and healing play devised by the children themselves. It is a crazy notion that we have, that children should be 'occupied' and 'busy' all the time. *There is nothing wrong with a thoughtful or resting child, nor one who is simply staring at the wonderful world around him.*

Children have a natural feeling for play and we are in danger of stifling this instinct with our adult ideas for structuring the play environment. They don't really need special sophisticated manufac-tured toys, activities and learning equipment in order to play. A ready-made plastic doll's house, complete in every lurid pink detail, leaves nothing to the imagination.

Joining in

Our involvement with our children is valuable when we give of ourselves and share a joint ven-ture or a game, but a parent who tries too hard, or reluctantly joins a young group, is not making much of a contribution. Remember, don't force it; it's OK to join in doing things you *like*, but don't strain tempers by feeling obliged to participate in every idea that comes up, especially those you loathe! Don't feel guilty about this, simply relax and enjoy the shared times you do have, feel good about other occasions when kids play alone or with others. You need quiet contemplative time too. Children instinctively know when you are forcing it, and when you are relaxed and happy.

In a survey of adult memories of childhood, very few people mentioned toys, and no one men-tioned that their moms kept a spotless kitchen floor! Memories were made of shared enjoyment and af-fection. It seems that the way to create happy mem-ories of childhood is to do what you enjoy together. An adult joining in reluctantly will be irritable and restless, so rather join in when you feel able to give of yourself and let that be a happy time.

Should I organise and plan ahead?

I don't think so!

Obvious organising for a morning or afternoon of successful playing or creative endeavour is often the least fruitful route. That is, if it is rigid planning. I find that the children's moods and the adult's plans seldom coincide. The day the parent decides on painting, the children can't stand the idea – they 'aren't in the mood'. Quick setting up and minimal clearing away will allow greater freedom of choice. Try to have the materials for different crafts and play stowed conveniently and simply. Leave a few possibilities open to them rather than plan a restrictive programme. Let the work develop according to their interest and experiments.

For a group of children who get on well together, parental presence might seem a nuisance – but then they might fight and fall apart so you should be ready to step in if needed with a *choice of positive ideas* to get things rolling again. It makes your life simpler if basic materials are to hand and you have thought out some possible alternatives. Have plenty of ideas ready – and be prepared to use none of them!

Always have a supply of paper of all sorts and sizes, plus pencils, felt tip pens, water colours or powder paints (pencil crayons are not my favourite as they encourage stiff stilted 'colouring in' style work), brushes of all sizes, tape and glue, string, cardboard, a magnifying glass, scissors, a magnet, modelling dough (in the fridge), a dressing up collection, scrap fabrics and basic cooking ingredients. You will then be able to offer a wide 'menu' of things to do.

Although I think that organising a rigid programme is seldom successful, you will want to have in mind a few ideas that can be used to calm things down a bit. Kids need no help in being wild or boisterous, but when this goes over the top a peaceful activity or quiet game can be soothing to all. Also if separating squabblers is necessary, this is easier if you can tempt a fighter with a new idea.

Teachers have found that playing classical music while children work at creative projects helps calm temperaments, and perhaps controls the noise level too. Choose carefully and note which pieces are successful. A rewarding summer art school project I know of had the kids note perfect in Vivaldi's *Four Seasons* as a side benefit!

All of us are at our most disruptive when bored or not sufficiently challenged. Children demonstrate this alarmingly quickly. We often underestimate what they can do and forget how fast they can master a new skill or game. Repeating it over and over again, they soon become 'ace' at it. For the type of child who is frequently disruptive, it helps to find something that stretches and stimulates him or her.

Can I make my child do what *I* want to do?

The only invariably successful method I know of getting a child to *want* to do what you feel like doing, is to start doing it yourself. When you seem remarkably absorbed, your child will ask you what you are doing and generally want to try it too. If you had said ten minutes before, 'I want to teach you how to do Japanese Origami,' I am prepared to lay bets that the reply would have been negative. But if you are totally absorbed folding paper and the child asks 'What are you doing?' you might reply casually, 'Making a jumping frog.'

Well, most adults of your child's acquaintance don't regularly make jumping frogs it is true, so now you have hooked him. The next thing you hear is likely to be, 'Can I do it too?'

This 'lead-in' pattern makes for fun and laughter and avoids confrontation, because, if your child does not join you, there has been no argument along the lines of . . . 'Why don't you want to do it now?' or (guilt-spreading) 'I've gone to so much trouble to get the paper for you.' Your child is free to do something else alongside you or simply watch, or perhaps wander off in search of a quite different activity. (No method is foolproof!) This leaves the door open for other days and other ideas. However, an argument about doing things together, or when *you* fancy doing them, leaves a nasty taste which must be an obstacle when you try again.

How to avoid the 'Perfect Parent' guilt syndrome

If you're any sort of normal parent, and there are many sorts of normal, then you'll be inundated with images of *better* parents: Supermoms, Daredevil Dads, parents who impart education to their offspring along with vitamins and clean socks in matching pairs. You may wonder why it is that you don't quite manage this. Trying to emulate these role models will lead you up a treacherous path. Exhaustion and feelings of inadequacy lie in wait here. Don't compete! Realise your personal limitations, cheat a little and relax!

The cheating involves training the children to do as much as possible for themselves. This strategy has long-term benefits and obviously takes time and patience. But, eventually, you will smugly point to their ability to cope, their independence, and their skill at fixing things up in a crisis.

Never force yourself to try to do everything, or be wonderfully organised if this is not you. Your kids don't know any other way remember; they are probably quite satisfied with you as you are . . . And if they aren't, there is not much they can do about it! Besides, perhaps there is no such animal as a perfect parent! It's joined the ranks of the unicorns, I think.

In setting up craft work, painting and modelling, a basic routine can be used. I keep an old plastic shower curtain, which rolls up out of the way when not in use but covers a generous area when spread out. If really messy, it can be hosed off outside. Keep protective covers like this, along with cast-off men's shirts (used as overalls), where the kids can find them. Teach them that no project can be started without this preliminary step.

Harder still is a clear-up routine, but you will need to be firm about this, or you will find yourself groaning each time they want to 'make' something. Establish from the start, with kids as young as five, that brushes must be washed clean, glue tightly sealed, scissors put away, etc, and show them what will happen if this is not done. They will certainly need your help, but you will not feel that you are slaving away alone.

After a game has been played it should not be mom who puts away the pieces. Have a competition to see who can pick up the most jigsaw puzzle pieces if you must, but put the onus on them to do it. Visiting kids can be told at the start of the visit that they can play with anything, but they are expected to put toys, puzzles and games back where they found them before leaving – and intact too!

How do I find time for all these activities?

Of course you don't set aside time for the sole purpose of playing tic-tac-toe with your child. The ideas here are for when you are together and you want to enrich that day, or pass the time in a line, or get through a boring journey. These diversions can be kept up your sleeve, as it were, and brought out when needed.

There is so much time when you are near a child, but doing some task yourself which is not engaging your mind. Guessing games can be played while you iron shirts or wash up. The car is not the only place where you will find yourself in an isolated bubble of self sufficiency. Many of the games which are listed as travel games are played in our family on a daily basis: walking to school, last thing before bedtime, when unexpectedly waiting about, and simply for the pleasure of it. Quality time is time shared and enjoyed, wherever and whenever you can.

I'm not creative . . .

Parents often say, 'I can't do these artistic things,' or 'I don't have the imagination . . . or the patience.' The wide range of suggestions in this book are offered so that you *can* find some area you can handle and enjoy (the key word). But there is no reason why your children should not be able to do the very thing you can't. A number of parents find that their kids are a whizz at things they themselves cannot do. Kids love being better than adults at anything, so this must give them a boost, and all you need do is be admiring and supportive. Provide the materials and the opportunities for painting and drawing for example, even if you can't draw a straight line. Leave them to get on with it.

The other side of the coin is the parent who is very good at doing something. This can be very disheartening for the child. He compares his amateur effort with the adult's successful one and may be frustrated. So if you are a wonderful artist or musician it is not always helpful to work alongside one another; it may be more tactful to take a back seat now and again.

What is worth buying?

With limited funds, most of us don't want to be pressured into the current toy fad, only to find that it is out of fashion a month later. We are looking for purchases that might offer hours of absorbed play. You can provide so much from objects you already have: the dressing-up box is an example of this . . . But there are a few techniques which require basic supplies, like paints and brushes, good pairs of scissors, construction sets, glue and books. If I were only able to give a small child one item, it would undoubtedly be a massive sack of good quality wooden blocks. These could become a new toy every day in the child's imagination. Some electronic toys are able to offer long-term enjoyment, with maths or spelling games graded to give greater challenge all the time, but others lose their novelty value after a few weeks.

Music-making instruments and homemade sound-producing inventions give long-term fun, as does every sort of ball you ever buy. Skipping ropes have given more than their fair share of value, and good quality paper has been a source of inspiration for artists and paper aeroplane experts alike. Modelling clay, homemade or plasticine, develops in its amorphous way into anything the child desires. Modern technology has made small tape recorders cheaper, and one of these can be used to explore the world of sound.

Every item bought for a child's use must be considered for safety. Use non-toxic pens and paints. Take care with adhesives.

safety in the play area

If young children are to play regularly in one area it pays to check that this place is as safe as you can make it. Consider it from the point of view of their height and level of curiosity. It is impossible to predict what children will do, nor prevent all accidents, but you certainly can make a play area safer.

- Remove all loose and excess length electric cords.

- Put filler plugs into empty sockets.

- Put a fireguard or screen in front of a heating appliance if it is not entirely safe. Preferably use another type.

- Never let a child touch water and electricity at the same time (or any adult for that matter).

- Never allow hot drinks – theirs or yours – in the play space. A cup of scalding coffee put down hastily while you answer the phone could be upturned in seconds.

- Poisonous cleaning fluids should never be kept within reach. And medicines likewise should be locked away.

- Windows should be checked. Children can climb on to sills very easily and could fall out.

- Venetian blinds have caused serious accidents as dangling cords become a noose. This applies to any looped curtain pulls; a child can put its head through a loop very easily.

- Children should not play and tumble about with chewing gum in their mouths; it can easily get stuck in the throat and cause a child to choke.

- Plastic bags are well known to be dangerous and could cause suffocation if a child puts a bag over its head, but few of us think of balloons as dangerous. When a balloon pops, little pieces of it can be put into a small mouth with dangerous consequences.

- Teach children how to handle scissors and knives with respect.

- Children must never go near a flame or any heat source without an adult in control.

- If you are doing sewing or woodwork with older children, have them take care with needles and sharp nails, and warn them of the dangers to toddlers and babies.

Eliminate dangers where you can. Sharp edges on low tables and furniture can be at the wrong height for your child. Provide hardwearing flooring, moppable surfaces and ample storage for toys and equipment. A first aid kit should be kept close at hand.

games
without
toys

Use these ideas whenever you are stuck with nothing to do and have no conventional toys with you. It is possible through these games to escape your surroundings and enter a world of imagination, laughter and invention as players of all ages use the language to entertain themselves and others. Games that require paper and pencil are marked, others can be done in the head.

Where possible, games are listed so that ideas for younger players are first, followed by those more complex games for older players. This system may be adapted for your own use, however, as many simple-seeming games may be played on a more sophisticated level.

word games

word collections

See how many words you can think of that are related to one another in some way. For a start, try to think of all the works that describe size, e.g. small, tiny, miniscule, or large, huge, gigantic . . . Another collection can be made of words describing the action of water – ripple, splash, drip, roar, trickle. You could go on and on. This can be done by simply calling out the words as you sit or walk together, or by writing them down against the clock.

• • • • •

two meaners

These are simply words that sound alike but have different meanings. As a family we have always called them Two Meaners. The hunt for these reaches a peak between the ages of five and seven, and kids will be making quite clever puns using them soon after learning to spot them. With a bit of thought you can find Three Meaners too. Pear, pair, pare, is one of these. Encourage children to think of as many as possible and let them try using them in sentences and generally enjoy the discovery.

When playing with very young children who do not read or spell well, concentrate on the sound of the letter rather than on accuracy with letters such as 'c' or 'k'. Say 'I spy something beginning with ''sh'' ' rather than 's', or 'Fetch me something beginning with ''th'' ', for example.

• • • • •

fetch me

This is fun for little players. Ask children to fetch you one object or a number of objects beginning with a certain letter. 'C' and they go hunting for clips, cap, carton, cushion, etc. As they get older, make it harder. Perhaps some rooms will be out of bounds for sanity?

• • • • •

I spy

This is such an old favourite that it hardly needs explaining. Yet I include it here for so many children and parents wrote to me listing it as a favourite. Make it more complex by including categories such as animal, vegetable or mineral. Players can ask the person who is 'spying' if the object falls into one of these. Some families allow those guessing to have only a limited number of questions, rather like Twenty Questions, or a fixed period of time after which they 'give up'.

Playing this while walking to school, I have been stumped by my daughter's 'a' for atmosphere (not entirely 'spyable') and 'v' for vehicles! From eight onwards children enjoy 'spying' rather subtle things like 'stripes' on fabrics in train carriages, or 'arrows' on a sign. This is a game which can range from the humdrum to the wildly imaginative, as 'it' says thoughtfully, 'I spy with my little eye . . . something beginning with . . .'

Books and authors:
Special Detective
by Ivor Klue

My Greatest Moment
by I. M. A. Phibba

buzz

This takes the previous game a step further. In the game of Buzz, the homonyms are used in a sentence, and each time one is used the player substitutes the word 'Buzz'. The other players must guess what the words are. 'I didn't Buzz that he was Buzz' (I didn't hear that he was here) and 'I didn't Buzz that he had said Buzz' (I didn't know that he had said no) are good examples to start off with. Where you can make sentences with three or more you are doing very well.

• • • • •

everlasting change

Popular with little ones, Everlasting Change is especially good for travelling torpor. In this game players must start a new word with the last letter (or sound, for very young players) of the word called out by the previous player. Each must take his or her turn promptly or be out. This leads to car, rat, tea.

To make it more of a challenge for older players, create categories, such as cars, or girls' or boys' names, and play as before. The first player calls out a name – 'Rebecca' – and the second must continue with a girl's name beginning with A: Amy = Yvonne = Elizabeth = Heather = Rachel.

association

Association requires players to say words very rapidly one after the other with no repetition. The first player says a word and the next must immediately say a word brought to mind by the first and associated with it. The next continues until someone is out, by repeating a word or by being unable to go.

• • • • •

opposites

These can be hunted down in much the same way as Two Meaners. It is amusing to have to sift through your vocabulary and find the correct opposite. Talking in opposites is great fun and very popular with eight to ten year olds, who love saying 'I hate you' to their best friends, then screaming with laughter. This speech can develop into a complicated secret language.

Play hunting for opposites as a guessing game, or write down lists for each other, swop lists and each try to get the opposites down on paper faster than the other player.

• • • • •

words within a word

Players try to make as many words as possible from the letters contained in one long word, within a given time limit. You may need a dictionary to settle disputes. Decide at the start whether you will allow plurals or not. Place names are not permitted.

In the variation called Constantinople, the players try to make as many words as they can beginning with 'C' using letters from this word. The time limit should be two minutes. Vary this by using the word Czechoslovakia!

How to Pass Exams
by I. D. Otte
Close to the Ground
by Neil Down
The Train is Coming
by Raoul Way

hangman

Universally played, this game has one player trying to guess the word thought up by his opponent before he is 'hanged'.

The first player thinks of a word and draws a dash for each letter in that word, i.e. – – – – –. The second player now tries to guess which letters go to make up that word. (The best idea is to begin with the five vowels.) If a letter guessed is correct, the first player writes it in its correct position; if it is not correct, he draws one part of the hangman diagram. The game continues until either the word is guessed or the hangman is completed.

• • • • •

general knowledge

A timeless game and one that many adults remember playing as kids.

On a piece of paper, draw up four or five columns. Head each of these with a category you have chosen: common ones are Countries of the World, Capital Cities, Plant Names, Rivers, Girls' or Boys' Names, Aeroplane or Car Makes, World Cup Players, Tennis Players, Breeds of Dogs, and others along these lines.

On another sheet of paper write the letters of the alphabet at random, scattering them over the page. With eyes closed, a player will let the pencil point fall on to a letter. Each player must quickly write one word beginning with this letter in each of the categories. The first to do so calls out 'Stop', and everyone must stop writing. Read out the words you have got to each other. Score two for a word nobody else has, one for a word somebody else has written down, and zero if you have no word in this category or if it is disqualified.

If the word you have written down is not truly in that category, then the other players can disqualify it. This happens if you have written down a city which is not a capital in the Capital Cities column.

The highest score wins. The winner chooses the next letter by closing his or her eyes and letting the pencil point drop to another letter on the alphabet sheet.

• • • • •

slogans

Collect a few well-known advertising slogans, proverbs or sayings, and write them out on a separate sheet of paper for each player, leaving out certain words as you do this. The winner is the first to fill in the missing words. Alternatively, play this non-competitively, all guessing together.

```
    D          O          G
   DO         OH         GO
  DIN        ODD        GET
 DULL       ONLY       GRIN
DRAIN      OTHER      GRA
```

pyramids

Choose a medium-sized word, write it out with each letter set apart across the top of a page. Beneath each letter players try to write a word beginning with the letter above. The words in the first row will be a two-letter word, the next row a three-letter word, the next four, and then five and so on if you can go any further. This game is played against the clock. Compare pyramids and count up the scores. Each word scores the number of letters it contains.

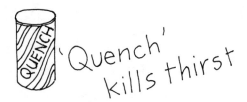

'Quench' kills thirst

the advertising game

This can be relatively sophisticated. The idea is to think up a name for a new product. Older players will define the market and discuss the connotations of a particular word and its appeal. It is important to strike the right note with the people who are likely to buy this product. It is not a competitive game (a relief to some), but a group game in which wit and ingenuity create entertainment for everyone.

If there are several players, divide into two groups and have each group think up products for the others to name. Then plan a campaign for this product, a slogan and an image. Suggestions might be a title for an album to be made by a well-known pop star, or a new canned drink on the market, a new cat food, or a new deodorant.

A variation of this game is listed in the travel section, in which players think up the names of businesses or shops they may be passing. Hairdressers called 'Curl up and Dye' are popular, as are words that clearly tell you what is being sold, like 'Slumberland' or 'Pizza Palace' or the plumbers' merchant called 'Everything on Tap'. 'Wooden Heart' and 'Pine Mine' are popular for wooden furniture stores, 'Bedlam' for beds and bed linen, and 'Gym and Tonic' was seen for a health and fitness centre.

As dry as a desert!

telegrams

All players invent imaginary telegrams, each word of which starts with the letters in one of the players' names. S U S A N could become 'Saw umbrella soaring above nanny'. If challenged you could say you were describing Mary Poppins! GEORGE might become 'Go early or risk going elsewhere'.

With older players, try choosing names of historic figures, and make up imaginary telegrams that could feasibly have come from them or have been sent to them.

WE INTEND NEVER STOPPING TILL OUR NEMESIS = Winston (Churchill)

DANGER ROUNDING AFRICA KILLS ELEVEN = (Francis) Drake

change

Start with any word that comes to mind and ask the next player to make a new word by changing or adding one letter. Play until you are unable to go any further; e.g. Wrong, wring, pring, prong, prone, crone, crane, crate, crater . . .

. . . . .

echo

Choose a word, then ask the next player to call out a rhyming word. Allow a few seconds. Continue until no more rhymes can be found. Count to ten slowly and if the next player has not thought of a word by then, he or she is out. Begin by calling out 'Give me a rhyme that sounds just like mine!' Then say the word.

scramble

The first player chooses a word and writes it down with the letters scrambled. The players have to try to work out what it is. To make it reasonably easy for young children, try to leave at least three letters of the word in order.

R S O N A E Y B L A = reasonably

• • • • •

YES and NO

In this variation of Yes and No it is forbidden to say either of these words in any form. Players talk to one another asking questions, trying to get their opponent to answer and slip up. It is not permitted to say the words **no**body or **yes**terday, etc, and players must think fast to get round the problem.

Other ways of using Yes and No appear in games such as Twenty Questions (opposite) when the answers can only be Yes or No, making it harder to guess the correct solution.

• • • • •

consequences

This can be played with words or pictures. In each case the method is the same.

Give each player a sheet of paper and a pencil. Near the top players must write the first few words of a story (or draw the head of any creature, animal or human). Then a small fold is made on each sheet so that this writing or drawing is covered. (With a drawing, leave two little lines to indicate where the neck finishes.) Pass the sheet to the person sitting on your left. Now write the next part of the story or draw from neck to waist. Fold as before and pass on. When the sheets are completed open them up for a good laugh. There can be as many as six steps if you like.

Older players can play Consequences with a theme. For them, prepare sheets in advance. On each sheet write the basics, which are filled in as the sheet is passed around. Some of these might be:

There was a boy called . . . .
There was a girl called . . . .
They met when . . . .
He said . . . .
She said . . . .
And the consequence was . . . .

Write a review of a movie
Give the title . . . .
Based on the book . . . .
By . . . .
Names of the stars . . . .
The plot was about . . . .
The acting was . . . .
The music was . . . .
The publication for which this review is being written is . . . .

• • • • •

There are many other ideas elsewhere in the book that require a piece of paper, from paper folding to making a floor plan of your room.

guessing games

the chair game

Place a chair in the middle of the room. A simple wooden dining chair is best. One player is chosen to go up to the chair and act out a scene, using the chair as the imaginary object it represents to him. The others try to guess what it is. The chair might be a car, a wheelbarrow, etc. It may be turned upside down or used in any position.

charades

Popular with all ages from about nine upwards, Charades gives an opportunity for taking centre stage, for acting flair, imaginative guesswork and fun with words.

For younger children, use words of two syllables if titles seem too hard. Send a team out of the room and help the second team to prepare their act. Words such as dustbin or pencil are suitable for young groups of around eight years old.

For older players, titles of books, plays, films or TV shows are chosen and acted out by one group while the other tries to guess it. Before you start, agree signs to show whether the title to be guessed will be that of a book, a film, etc. These signs must be understood by all. Next, you will need a signal to show how many words make up this title; the most common is to hold up the right number of fingers. This is followed by a sign to indicate that you are dealing with the first word, and how many syllables this word has. Teams have enjoyed acting out *Playschool*, *Wind In The Willows*, *The Lion, the Witch and the Wardrobe*.

paper charades

In this version of charades the players in one team think of a title of a film, book or play and draw pictures illustrating the literal meaning of the words. The other team tries to guess what it is. This can be played with two players or an entire party.

20 questions

The players have twenty opportunities to ask useful questions in order to identify an answer. This may be played as 'What work do I do?' or 'Who am I?', or even 'How did I get here?' Fanciful and way-out modes of transport like chariots jostle with space rockets in the minds of the players as they guess how 'it' got here.

If you want to make things harder, combine this game with Yes and No (opposite), so that 'it' can only answer Yes or No to each of the twenty questions. The questions then have to be carefully phrased to get the most out of each one. For example, if you were trying to guess the answer to 'How did I get here?' you might ask if 'its' transport had wheels. An answer of 'Yes' or 'No' would tell you something useful.

can you guess the number?

Speedy work is needed here to guess or calculate the answers to a set of prepared questions. Players may not leave the room. Set a time limit.

The sort of questions to prepare are:

How many floorboards are there in the room?

How many tiles are there in the bathroom?

How many grains of rice are there in a table-spoon? (To avoid conflict, have this spoon filled and visible.)

What is the length of this room?

How long is Suzie's hair?

How many sweets or potato chips are there in this packet?

How many windows are there in this house or apartment?

If your shoelaces were all laid end to end, how long would they be?

Hand out a tape measure so that the players can check the answers afterwards.

pencil and paper games

Pencil and paper games can be played at home, while travelling, when you are stuck in a line, while you're sick – in fact they can be played anywhere.

• • • • •

cartooning

This can be played as a competition or simply as a form of doodling. Give the players a basic pattern – in this case three small round or oval shapes – and let them see how they can change the expression of this face, for face it is, by placing eyebrows, pupils, mouth, eyelids, moustache, beard or even hair on to this simple framework.

comic strips

Well known to us all! But drawing your own comic strip is quite a challenge. First draw your strip, or series of three or four boxes. Start with a simple story and try to break down the action into three or four main parts to fill the frames. To begin, try to draw the action so that no words are needed. Later a bubble or caption may be helpful.

• • • • •

dots *(2 players)*

There are three games to play on a grid of dots: Boxes, Maze and Squares. For all these you begin

by drawing a grid of evenly spaced dots, about ten by ten.

1 Dotty Boxes In the first game each player has a turn in which to draw a line directly joining two of the dots. (They must be dots next to one another.) When a player joins the fourth side of a square he or she scores that square and writes their initials inside it. This player then has another turn. Players must try to avoid giving one another opportunities to make up squares because, as the game progresses, you can make long runs of squares simply by using your extra turn after each square is completed. Careful planning is needed early in the game. The player with the highest number of squares at the end is the winner.

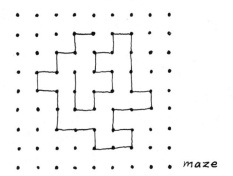

maze

2 Maze In the game of Maze each player again makes a line between two adjacent dots, but now the object is to draw lines which do not touch or cross any path and so block the maze created. Each new line, however, must join an existing line without blocking another route. The first to make this mistake, or be unable to go, is out.

3 Squares This is played with the squares already drawn in the field of dots. This time the object is to gain as many squares as you can in a vertical, horizontal or diagonal run. Players take turns to write their initials in a single square at a time. The person gaining the last square of a run scores the entire run, the highest score wins.

squiggles

One player draws a vague squiggle on a sheet of paper and the next must turn it into a picture.

• • • • •

tic-tac-toe

An old stalwart, universally played. It is included here with paper and pencil games, but could equally well be scratched in the dust or on the sand.

One player (O) places his O in a box; the other player (X) puts his X in another. The turns continue. The object is to get three of your own symbols in a row, vertically, horizontally or diagonally, while being on the alert to defend boxes where your opponent is aiming for a threesome. Try to guess his intentions and block him.

• • • • •

number trios

Draw the usual tic-tac-toe grid. At the top of the grid write the numbers 1–9 in a line. There are two players and each in turn uses one of these numbers by writing it in a square. As a number is used, cross it out on the top line. No number can be used twice. The object is to get a run of three, in which the numbers are in a sequence – 123, or 876, or 369 are examples of runs. Your run can be in any direction, vertical, horizontal or diagonal.

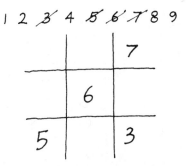

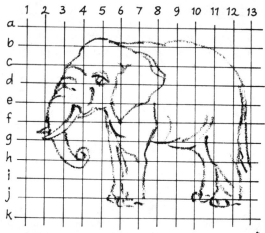

remote control drawings

Make someone else do an identical drawing to yours without seeing your drawing first!

To do this you need to make two grids, one each. (You could take a short cut and use squared paper.) The smaller the squares, the more accurate the result. Number the vertical lines and give letters of the alphabet to each of the horizontal lines. Draw your picture on your grid. Without letting your partner see your drawing, give instructions using co-ordinates so that his or her pencil moves in one direction at a time, slowly re-creating your picture. Instructions will be 'draw a line from 1b to 3d' or 'from 6j to 12k'.

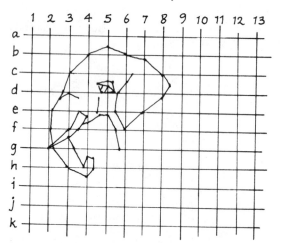

Across

2. – – – – or swim
4. Before noon
5. Mother Hubbard searched for one
7. Try peeping
8. Donkey?
10. Not the whole

Down

1. Sunbathe to get one
2. Frozen flakes
3. Necessities
6. Let fall
8. Pretending play
9. Shines upon us

make your own crossword puzzle

Draw a square the overall size of your puzzle. Draw in the smaller squares, then write in the words that will form the answers to your puzzle — make the words going in both directions interlock where possible. Fill in the blanks as black squares. Now number in a sequence the first letter of all the words that go across and go down. Carefully prepare clues for each word and list these clues in two columns headed Down and Across.

Now prepare a blank version of your puzzle with empty squares where your words were and fill in the black squares as before. Copy out the clues beneath and you are ready to find a victim.

hands and fingers

You may not have conventional toys with you, but as all babies will have discovered, hands and fingers are fascinating and conveniently with you wherever you are. Keep a few of these ideas up your sleeve for instant entertainment at difficult moments.

painted faces

Paint a face on your child's hand in a position where the movement of the hand will make the face appear to smile or frown. The face may be that of a dragon opening and shutting a fearsome array of teeth.

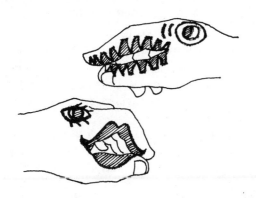

finger guessing games

These are ideal for toddlers and pre-schoolers. Hiding a couple of fingers, show the child how many remain. The child must work out how many are hidden. There are many variations on this, the simplest starter is to use only one hand at first so that the child is adding or subtracting numbers up to five.

traditional finger rhymes

Here is the church,
Here is the steeple
Open the doors . . .
And here are the people.

Here is the beehive,
Where are the bees?
Hiding away where nobody sees.
Watch them come creeping
Out of their hive,
1 and 2 and 3, 4, 5.

finger puppets

1 Draw a face or a creature on your finger with a ballpoint pen, and tell a little story with the finger acting as a puppet. It is fun to try to co-ordinate two or more finger puppets talking animatedly together!

2 From a piece of card, make a cut-out puppet, fold back where the legs begin, cut two holes and place your fingers in these to form legs. For a four legged animal, your fingers work hard to do the walking!

shadows on the wall

Recognisable creatures can be seen in the shadows your hand makes on a wall when you carefully arrange the fingers and palm. Fingers meeting thumb, then opening and closing will make a quacking duck when placed sideways against the light. You can, with a little ingenuity, also make cats with pricked ears if you bend fingers down but keep thumb and little finger up; or try a dog made by holding second finger and little finger upwards to form ears, and point the two middle fingers and thumb forward to form the opening and closing mouth.

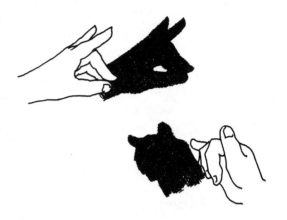

scissors, paper or stone

This ancient game is played with the hand representing one of the three elements in the game. It is a form of power struggle, if you like, for the stone can make the scissors blunt, scissors can cut paper, and paper can wrap up a stone.

Played in pairs, each player makes a signal with the hand. On the count of three these hand signals are displayed. If both sides give the same gesture, the game is a draw. The winner of each round scores a point.

The signal for stone is a clenched fist. That of scissors has the second and third fingers extended like a pair of open scissor blades. The signal for paper has the hand flat with all the fingers extended as though you were about to shake hands with someone.

Hide your hands behind your back to prepare the signal and bring them out on the call hoping to be able to better your opponent's choice.

clapping and clicking games

Traditional playground games are passed on to younger children as a matter of course.

Clap hands, clap opposite hands with your partner, clap your own hands then slap your knees.

Clap hands then click fingers in a rhythm. On each click the next player calls out a word that is associated with the previous one. See Association, page 17.

There are traditional playground rhymes chanted with clapping or clicking games. The majority of these have some element which is considered a bit naughty or revolting. This seems to give them a little edge of excitement! They also contain crazy ideas linked to improbable situations. In one, elephants jump ever so high, and in another loaves of bread are bought at the Chinese restaurant. Schoolchildren know many of these and, if asked, can trot out a large repertoire. Use these for clapping and skipping games as well as to while away waiting time. They all have a repetitive beat and a sing song quality that makes them easy to remember and adaptable to various games. But above all it is their complete naïvety that sets genuine children's rhymes apart.

I went to a Chinese restaurant
To buy a loaf of bread, bread, bread
They wrapped it up in a five dollar bill
And this is what they said, said, said.
My name is
Elvis Presley
Girls are sexy
Sitting in the back seat
Drinking Pepsi.
Nudge, nudge, wink, wink 'How d'you like it
    baby!'

This last done with much acting and
hip swinging!

Clapping and chanting, from a school playground
in London despite its USA sound.

Miss Mary Mack, Mack, Mack
All dressed in black, black, black
With buttons, buttons, buttons,
All down her back, back, back.
She asked her mother, mother, mother,
For fifty cents, cents, cents,
To see the elephants, elephants, elephants,
Jump over the fence, fence, fence.
They jumped so high, high, high,
They reached the sky, sky, sky,
And didn't come back, back, back
Till the fourth of July, July, July.
July can walk, walk, walk,
July can talk, talk, talk,
July can eat, eat, eat,
With a knife and fork, fork, fork.

Clap hands on knees.
Clap hands crossed on chest.
Clap hands together.
Click fingers of both hands three times for 'Mack,
Mack, Mack.
Repeat from beginning, in any order.

My boyfriend gave me an apple
My boyfriend gave me a pear
My boyfriend gave me a kiss on the lips
And threw me down the stair.

I gave him back his apple
I gave him back his pear
I gave him back his kiss on the lips
And threw him down the stair.

I threw him over London
I threw him over France
I threw him over Africa
And now he's with his aunts.

Played with three girls, clapping.
Shades of Superwoman!

Here is the sea, the watery sea
Here is the boat and here is me
All the little fishes down below
Wriggle their tails and away they go.

things around the house

name hunt

Teach a child to hunt for names of friends and relatives in the 'phone book. This can be made into races against the clock, or simply treated as a useful skill. From about the age of eight this is a versatile game that can be of real benefit.

•••••

word hunt

Using a dictionary is marginally more difficult than a 'phone book, but equally interesting to young readers. There are many dictionaries prepared for children, but somehow we never seem to have one on hand and have always used an adult one. Kids find strange words amusing and will make rude jokes about every possible word if they are going through 'that' phase.

•••••

card palace

Using an old pack of cards, build an amazing construction by balancing the cards one against the other. One of the easiest methods is to start by leaning two cards against each other. Then when they are stable do the same with another pair next to them. Place a 'roof' card, horizontal, on the two peaks you have built. Continue upwards and outwards. Building up on these can be a test of skill and shallow breathing.

sports commentating

Using an old hairbrush as an imaginary microphone, one child commentates on the football on TV (sound turned off), or on any other interesting event such as two brothers wrestling on the floor.

•••••

string

Taking up almost no space, a piece of string could become a child's trusted friend with many games and tricks to be played using it. Take it with you on a journey or when you might have to hang around. Frequently people can show you new versions of the old and well-known games and tricks. Naturally, you will not be giving string to a child who is too young to understand that it must not be put around his neck.

> 'I had a little string
> It was no good at all.
> I went to look for more string
> To make a string ball.'

These are the first words in a book for small children, *A Big Ball of String* (Marion Holland, Random House, 1958), that has delighted us for nineteen years. In this story, the boy gathers string from everywhere and finally joins the pieces up to form a string ball. With this huge ball of string he makes 'machines' of every kind imaginable while he is supposedly in bed with a bad cold. He plans to stay in bed (finally, when he has tied everything up) so that he can manipulate a toy mouse to tempt his cat in, and use a pulley which will bring his dressing gown towards him — among other examples of his skill with string.

The sense that anything is possible with

string has inspired many crazy constructions. Amazing string contraptions acted as a burglar alarm in my son's room, bringing down on my head old tennis shoes and upturned boxes of gunge. Bells rang and a general fearsome racket made me quickly turn tail. Inventive? Most definitely!

The art of string weaving, games and figure-making has flowered all around the world. In primitive cultures grasses, horse hair and sinew were used as quick fingers wove intricate and often symbolic figures. Children all over the world play Cat's Cradle with slight variations. These string figures, as they are called, developed as part of the culture of many peoples spread right across the globe – from the Eskimos to the people of the South Pacific.

a standard starting position

Keep a simple loop of string in your pocket and practise often.

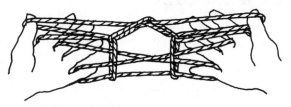

from the Eskimos: 'The Siberian House'

waiting around

Waiting around produces games of a similar type in most kids. If there are paving slabs or squares of flooring they will be tempted into hopping, jumping and not touching the lines without any guidance from an adult! Another popular challenge is to balance on the lines: walking along them and only placing their feet exactly on the lines.

This can be varied by balancing first on one foot, then on tip-toe. Positions of difficulty can be attempted: standing still on a line with one leg in the air and waving both arms without falling or wobbling off it. This game can be created in a room using a tile or a floorboard crack or a ribbon for a line.

parent's dream

How long can a child go without making any sound whatever? This is timed on a stopwatch.

Children could be encouraged to try to sneak up on you or each other silently, without knocking furniture or making any shuffling or stifled chuckling sounds. You sit facing away from them and do not look round unless a sound is heard. This game was a favourite of Maria Montessori, who felt children became alert and agile as they discovered their capacities and perfected their achievements. The sneaking up soon becomes fast soundless running as the children gain control of their movements.

• • • • •

line maths

Children can work out how many people there are in a line, and the average number of minutes taken to serve or see each person. They can then be occupied counting how many people are ahead of you in the line and multiplying by the average time taken for each person. The result will probably make you give up waiting and simply walk off into the blue with your human calculators.

counting games

Other line games based on counting and mathematical sets are most suitable for children in the first year or two of school. In these, children count how many people have black shoes on or wear jeans, and they compare one set to another. Are there more people wearing jeans than not wearing jeans? Are there more people wearing black shoes than brown? If so, how many more? Thus occupied, they are not looking to you with whining requests every minute and you are free to stand and dream or simply switch off, a rare gift to a parent of young children! I have been forced to come to suddenly when the game switched to listing amazingly personal features such as double chins and moustaches, ladies' included!

• • • • •

treasure hunt

This is another game you can play while waiting in a line. It is played mentally and no object is really hidden. However, the first player mentally hides the treasure in a place all players can actually see, and the others have to guess where this is. The hiding place should be unlikely and funny; the answers may be 'hot' or 'cold' and the guesses wild. Watch out for cheating!

• • • • •

singing

Finally of course, waiting around is much improved by singing. Provided you're waiting in a suitable place, this is the easiest way to have fun.

brainteasers

Get your family's brains to tangle with a few riddles, codes, paradoxes and general brainteasers. These will wake up all those bored brain cells! Once these ones are solved, set to work devising new ones. There is no upper age limit to puzzles; many adults love them, others are completely stumped by them. These are well-known examples that have been around for years; it would be inventive to produce your own.

Introduce brainteasers by way of a challenge ('I bet you can't decode this message') or fantasy idea ('Wouldn't you like to be able to send messages in a secret code?'). Once you have mastered a couple of codes, sending messages and decoding them is something to do on a train or during any boring wait. A family could develop its own private code – very useful for special communications! Good luck!

number sequences and codes

Teach a child to decode a message, spot a number sequence or work out what comes next and he or she will soon outwit you at this game. Patterns of numbers or letters can convey messages and form a secret code. Boring odd moments when there is nothing to do can be used to devise new codes or to prepare number sequences for others to try to work out.

• • • • •

simple number sequences

First practise number sequences:

1, 2, 4, 7, 11, —, —, —

Study this sequence closely and try to work out what number comes next. What are the next three numbers?

Answer on page 38.

For younger children, simply counting in tens or odds and evens is fun as they become more familiar with numbers. Gradually more complex patterns can be tried out. Use the same counting patterns backwards from 100.

Here are some simple number sequences:

1. 2, 5, 8, 11, —, —, —
2. 1, 2, 4, 8, —, —, —
3. 30, 27, 24, 21, —, —, —
4. 80, 40, 20, 10, —, —, —
5. 12, 11, 16, 15, 20, —, —, —

Answers on page 38.

secret combination lock

Imagine you are faced with a secret combination lock. To open it you must work out what the missing numbers are:

Answer on page 38.

• • • • •

grid number sequence

This grid is a number sequence too. Can you complete it?

15	6
19	8
25	11
7	2
?	4
13	5

9	3
?	9
27	12
5	1
17	7
?	10

Answer on page 38.

magic squares

This is a teaser for children over ten. A Magic Square is a well-known arrangement of numbers. It is a grid in which the sum of every row, column and diagonal comes to the same number when added.

Magic Square No 1:

In this 3 × 3 grid, use the numbers 1, 2, 3, 4, 5, 6, 7, 8, 9, to make the sum of each row, column and diagonal add up to 15.

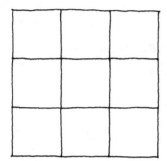

Magic Square No 2:

In this larger grid, use the numbers 1–16 and make the sum of every row, column and diagonal equal 34.

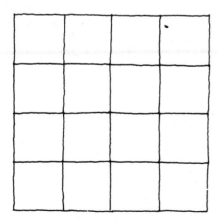

Answers on page 38.

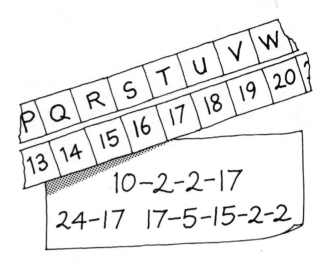

secret codes

These are handy for a club or for sending private messages between friends.

1 One of the simplest secret codes is to allocate numbers to the letters of the alphabet. This is easy if you write out the alphabet on a long strip of squared paper, repeating the whole thing again when you come to Z. On another similar strip, write out the numbers from 1–26 twice. Place these two strips alongside each other and line up the squares. To begin with you may use the number 1 for the letter A. In this case your two strips will simply be one above the other with the letter A above the number 1.

If your code is to be more secretive, try moving the strips along in opposite directions and choose some other letter to be number 1. Arrange your strips so that the numbers and letters correspond to your new plan. For example, if H is to be the new number 1, line up the number strip beneath the alphabet strip with the 1 directly beneath the H. You will see that all the letters now have new numbers and that 26 is G.

2 Another fast and simple code is to displace the letters of the alphabet by one place. For example A=B, B=C and so on.

3 A more complex code is based on times tables, and a grid is used. Write down the message and count the number of letters contained in it. 'The Martians have landed' has 21 letters: 21 = 7 × 3. Now write out this message in three columns of seven letters each, beginning at the top left hand corner and writing downwards rather than across.

```
T I E
H A L
E N A
M S N
A H D
R A E
T V D
```

Now write this out as **TIE HAL ENA MSN AHD RAE TVD**. Your message is ready to send.

If you have a message which does not divide up exactly add z to the end of the message to make the number of letters more suitable. 'When will you attack' is 17 letters, + Z = 18.

```
W L T
H L T
E Y A
N O C
W U K
I A Z
```

WLT HLT EYA NOC WUK IAZ.

Grids work well when they are of a squarer shape, i.e. four rows of five, and the 'words' created on the grid can be written out separately.

'When you give the signal' = 20.

```
W O E I
H U T G
E G H N
N I E A
Y V S L
```

WOEI HUTG EGHN NIEA YVSL.

• • • • •

code cracking

To crack a code, if you don't know the secret system, look for the most commonly used letters. Study the message carefully and note the letter or number that is most often repeated. Try to decide whether this could be an I or an E. We know that E is often followed by R or D at the end of a word, so this could be a clue when you find the two symbols often occurring together. If, for example, the writer of the message has used the simple displacement method (code 2), he will have used the letter F for E throughout. F is not such a common letter and you would notice if it was popping up far more often than you might expect. It should alert you to the possibility that it might be used as an E.

Always begin by looking for pattern in the jumble of letters in front of you.

code 4

A	J	R
B	K	S
C	L	T
D	M	U
E	N	V
F		W
G	O	X
H	P	Y
I	Q	Z

Now read the message;

paradox

A paradox is anything which appears to be true but is actually false – or which appears to be false but is actually true. Many brainteasers take this form. They are often infuriating but will certainly keep the mind intrigued.

paradox 1

One of the most famous examples of a paradox is the one about the man who says: 'I am lying.'

Is his statement true? If so, then he is lying and his statement is false.

Is his statement false? If so, then he is lying and his statement is true.

When you have got your minds twisted around that one, and everyone understands the nature of a paradox, you might like to try a few more or make up your own. Here are some more:

paradox 2

Two fathers and two sons leave town. This reduces the population of the town by three. False?

Well, if the trio that leave town are father, son and grandson then the statement is true.

paradox 3

The next is a little more difficult. This concerns a bookworm eating its way through some thick volumes. The worm starts at the outside of the front cover of volume I of a certain set of books. He eats his way to the outside of the back cover of volume III. If each volume is one inch thick, he must travel three inches in all. True?

False. The bookworm only travels one inch. Have a look at this:

the worm's journey

paradox 4

Charles Dodgson, otherwise known as Lewis Carroll, author of *Alice In Wonderland*, was a mathematician. He is responsible for this paradox:

'We can agree can we not, that the better of two clocks is the one that more often shows the correct time? Now suppose we are offered a choice of two clocks, one of which loses a minute a day, while the other does not run at all. Which one shall we accept?

'Common sense tells us to take the one which loses a minute a day, but, if we are to stick to our agreement, we shall have to take the one which doesn't run at all. Why?'

Answer: the clock that loses a minute a day,

once properly set, will have to lose 12 hours, or 720 minutes, before it is right again. It will take 720 days to lose 720 minutes. In other words, it is correct only once about every two years. But the clock that doesn't run at all is correct twice a day!

• • • • •

paradox 5

Finally, a different type of problem.

Three men had dinner in a restaurant. The bill came to $30.00. They each paid $10.00. The waiter took the money to the cashier and was told that there had been a mistake. The bill only came to $25.00, so he was sent back with $5.00.

On the way he realised that it was going to be difficult to divide the $5.00 between the three men, and that the men did not know the actual amount of the bill anyway, and that they would be glad of any return of money. So he slipped $2.00 into his pocket and gave each man $1.00 back.

Now each of the men paid $9.00. Three times 9 = 27. The waiter had $2.00 in his pocket. $27 + 2 = 29, and the men originally handed over $30.00. Where is the other dollar?

Too little or too much attention to detail misleads!

paradox 6

Another of this type (but easier) is the one about the lady in the jeweller's shop.

A scatterbrained young lady went into a jeweller's shop and picked out a ring worth $1.00. She paid for it and left. She appeared at the shop the next day and asked if she might exchange it for another. This time she picked one worth $2.00, thanked the jeweller sweetly and started to leave. He naturally demanded the other $1.00 but she pointed out that she had paid him $1.00 the day before and had returned a ring worth $1.00 and therefore she owed him nothing! Whereupon she stalked out of the shop and left him counting wildly on his fingers.

puzzles
• • • • • • • • • • • • • •

the rosebush puzzle

A gardener in a park had seven rosebushes. He wanted to make the most of them, so he decided to plant them in a pattern that would give six rows of three. Can you work out how he arranged them?

Answer on page 38.

matchstick puzzles

1 Using twelve sticks, lay out four squares. The challenge is to take away only two sticks but to leave two complete squares.

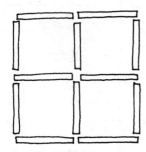

2 Using seventeen sticks, lay out six squares in two rows of three. The challenge is to take away only six sticks to leave two squares.

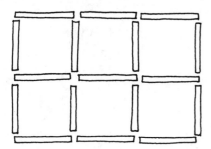

3 Lay six matches vertically side by side. Give the player an additional five. The challenge is to make only nine with what you've got.

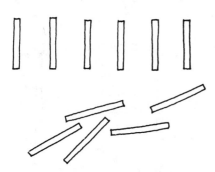

4 Can you re-arrange these matchsticks to make the sum correct?

Answers on pages 38 and 39.

Can you make up your own matchstick puzzles?

• • • • •

coin puzzle

For this you will need ten coins, stones or counters. Lay them in a triangle as shown in the diagram. The challenge is this: you may move only three coins, and this must reverse the direction of the triangle and make it point downwards.

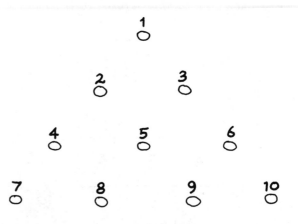

answers

Simple number sequence, page 32
To the first number, add one; to the second, add two; then three to the next and so on.

1. + 3 each time
2. × 2 each time
3. − 3 each time
4. ÷ 2 each time
5. − 1, + 5 each time.

Secret combination lock, page 32
Opposite segments add up to 16.

Grid number sequence, page 32
Each pair of numbers is completed by multiplying the one in the right hand box by 2 and adding 3 to give the number in the left hand box. The missing numbers are therefore 11, 21, and 23.
Example: 4 × 2 = 8 + 3 = 11.

Magic square no 1, page 33

4	9	2
3	5	7
8	1	6

Magic square no 2, page 33

16	3	2	13
5	10	11	8
9	6	7	12
4	15	14	1

Rosebush puzzle, page 36

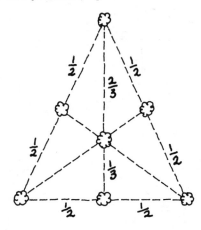

Matchstick puzzles, page 37

1

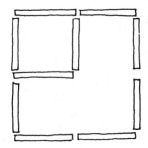

2

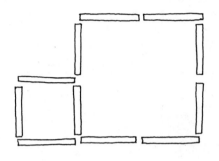

Coin puzzle, page 37

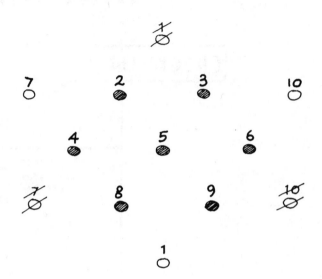

3

Number 7 is moved up
next to number 2.
Number 10 is moved up
next to 3.
1 is brought down
to make the point
below 8 and 9.

4

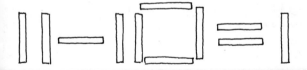

OR

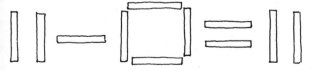

travelling

CHECK IN

by car, train and plane

Even a two-hour car trip can have the whole family bickering and the driver desperate, long waits for delayed trains are a regular occurrence. And travelling by air with small children or a baby can be a nightmare. Why do it? Well, if we must, and of course we often have to, we can improve our chances with a few tried and tested suggestions from veteran parent travellers.

Think about bringing along some of the following:

● Story and music cassettes; with personal cassette and headphones for train or plane. Local libraries stock ones your child may not have heard before, or record your own favourites doing various voices yourself beforehand for an unbeatable effect.

● Magic slates, travel games such as Connect 4, Travel Chess and Solitaire.

● Cheap jotting pads and pencils.

● Sticky stars and shapes, gummed labels and dots of different colours, found in office stationery shops.

- Moist towelettes, toilet paper or kitchen towel for mopping up and absorbing spills.

- Mini puzzles carried in a matchbox or empty 35 mm film container, available in shops, or make your own by cutting up a postcard or Christmas card.

  A clipboard for writing or drawing on will pack flat into a backpack (the best way for kids to carry their travel gear, hands are free).

- Dot-to-dot books of puzzles and crosswords for older travellers. Good paperback novel for eight years upwards.

- Three-year-olds enjoy cardboard shapes which they must identify with their eyes closed. Include a triangle, square and circle and let them feel and guess. Put these into an envelope.

- Small cartons of juice with their own straws.

- Books to help you identify birds, flowers, architecture and animals, which could live permanently in the car. Most highway maps include views of traffic signs which kids love to look up.

  Fruit, raisins and cookies will leave less mess than potato chips which shatter all over the back seat and stick to the upholstery. Chocolate always melts in whatever form you choose.

- Magic blanket or favourite teddy or doll (we have to take a little case of clothes for her too), and a couple of adored familiar items to help a toddler settle in on the holiday.

- Pattern books of geometric designs to work at with felt pens allow scope for personal design and flair. Drawing books and drawing pencils.

car sickness

Looking down and reading makes some children car sick, so encourage this child to look up and forward and keep attention focused. Mild nausea can be helped by sucking hard candy, or some prefer a salty cracker. There are those who swear by fizzy drinks, particularly flat coke. If your child is a really bad case, carry travel sickness tablets. In all cases, having fresh air passing through the car will help. Keep a couple of plastic bags handy if the unavoidable happens, and be ready to mop up with paper towel and moist towelettes or wipes.

long journeys

A change of clothing is a great help on long train, plane or car journeys with little ones. Try to provide meals or drinks at roughly the same times your child is accustomed to them, despite having to change your watch to local time.

Eye shades, saved from previous plane journeys, are useful on any form of transport to help a child drift off to sleep. Some like to listen to music on headphones at the same time. A small blanket is a must for a toddler. Encourage each child to pack his or her own travel gear in a small rucksack, easily carried and leaving hands free and the child walking upright, not leaning to one side.

travel games

There are many other ideas elsewhere in this book that can be used when travelling. Look through **Games without toys**, read about stories in **Fun and fantasy**, try games with rhythm and rhyme from **Sound and Rhythm** and drawing ideas.

• • • • •

animal alphabet

One player starts this game by naming an animal that begins with the letter "a." Players then take turns naming other animals whose names begin with an "a," such as "aardvark," "armadillo," and "ant." When a player cannot think of another "a" animal, he receives a strike against him, and then begins the list of animal names beginning with "b." Players continue through the alphabet, dropping out of the game when they have received three strikes. The last player left wins.

• • • • •

car maths

For a little mental arithmetic on the highway, players add up the number of cars that approach and take away the number of cars that pass you. Alternatively, add up all the trucks you see and take away all the vans.

Counting cars of different colours can reveal which are the most popular colours. In hot countries, the favourite is usually white or a light shade; whereas in cold countries you are more likely to see dark colours. It is interesting to talk about why this is so.

postcard jigsaw puzzle

Prepare a puzzle in advance by cutting up an old postcard. Pop the pieces into an envelope and use this lightweight, flat, convenient puzzle to entertain a child while waiting around or travelling in a train or plane. Take it along on a car journey for use at an unscheduled stop or at the destination.

• • • • •

shopping list

Players draw up a shopping list and, as shops go by, they try to spot places where the items on the list might be found and bought. The first to complete the list is the winner. Charges of cheating are avoided if the list is written out and ticked off.

• • • • •

fanciful shopping

This is a different game, also based on shopping. The first player says, 'Mrs Brown went to town and bought . . .' adding one item. Each player in turn repeats the whole sentence with a complete list of everything already bought, in the right order, and then adds his own item to the end of the list. No repeats or omissions allowed.

An imaginative variation on this is played using characters from books or movies. They naturally buy items related to the story – things they will need to solve mysteries, find missing treasure, or sail across oceans. For example, 'Alice in Wonderland put in her bag . . .' or 'Paddington bear put in his case . . .', 'Nancy Drew collected together . . .'

snap

Ever popular, all forms of snap are known to all forms of child. In this version you pick an object, perhaps a car, choose make and colour. You all look for this exact car and shout 'snap' on seeing it. The first to shout is the winner.

• • • • •

categories

For this a category is chosen, e.g. flowers, cars, colours, countries or rivers (suitable for the age of the players). Choose a letter of the alphabet. All players must think of items in the category chosen beginning with the letter selected. The older the players, the higher the number of cars, flowers, etc you can call for. In a mixed age group, allow little players to think of one, and older players several, keeping the game evenly matched in this way. No repetition is allowed.

• • • • •

quiz

If you are planning a journey in advance and the guide books are strewn all over the table, this could be a useful moment to draw up a quiz for children to complete on or after the journey.

Questions can relate to where you are going, methods of transport, changes in time, directions, wind, weather, local customs, foods, history and general interest. Mix obvious questions with others which will require a little detective work. Returning from a holiday, suggest that children might make each other lists of quiz questions – letting tired parents off the hook.

If you like the idea but can't see yourself drawing up a quiz, many local tourist authorities have quiz sheets, and so do many museums and places of interest.

mock mike

The mock microphone is a hairbrush or similar shaped object held in the hand. Looking out of the window, players have to give a smooth commentary on what can be seen. Witty and pithy please, no repetition, no 'ums' and 'ahs' allowed. Try to be as professional as possible. The commentary could take the form of a documentary on the main sights, or history of the town, or use imaginary moments in historic battles as knights come galloping over the hill. The first to falter or repeat must hand over the mike to the next player, who must begin to speak *at once*. A player is considered out if their imaginary scene is too improbable – steeds galloping over the Arctic, for example. The scene must be likely and historically fairly accurate, though it can be amusing.

• • • • •

now

Played in the car, this game must not involve or disturb the driver! Pick an object in the distance, a bridge perhaps. The passengers shut their eyes and shout out 'Now' when they think it is overhead. The person who estimates this most accurately is the winner.

• • • • •

how fast are we travelling?

In this game players must estimate the speed of the car without seeing the speedometer. Study the map. Choose a landmark a certain distance from where you are now – this must be a measurable distance, three miles is about right. Using a watch, players time how long it takes to reach this chosen landmark, and work out the speed from that.

design ideas

design a flag

Taking into account all the early influences and historical factors, flora and fauna, children might like to design a flag for the place you are visiting.

. . . . .

design a postcard

Having seen the local sights, and taking into account the taste of the tourists, design a best-selling card for this place. Children might choose to design a poster, using the larger scale this offers.

design a stamp

Special stamps are issued to commemorate particular occasions, historic events, or famous people. Look at a selection of U.S. stamps together, then children might want to try to design something striking and relevant to fit into the tiny space found on a stamp.

maps

dealing with a map

Being able to read a map effectively is a valuable and essential skill. It is worth putting aside a quiet moment at home to familiarise all the travellers, old and young, with the route you intend to take. Navigators will need to be able to search for the location in the index, and then interpret the numbers listed after the place name. Show them how these numbers relate to the page number if it is a map in page form, and then explain the co-ordinates which follow. Within the square indicated by these guides they will find the place they are looking for. It is amazingly easy when you know how, yet I know many adults who have a fear of maps and shy away from using one.

Mark the route you will be following either with a coloured marker, or on a separate sheet of paper. Mark major turn-offs and landmarks. Many journeys are made more interesting for children if they navigate, hunting for these signposts and landmarks, or trying to locate your position on the map. It is useful to have a second map as the kids usually refuse to surrender theirs to the front seat when you're lost and insist on sorting it out themselves, regardless of gas cost or wear and tear on the nerves.

Detailed topographical maps show rises in the ground, and all local buildings. Churches can be easily spotted.

. . . . .

navigate in town

Boring city car journeys in heavy slow moving traffic have often been made more bearable when the navigation has been left to my small assistant in the back seat. Early efforts were helped by my choosing routes I already knew reasonably well, and by getting her to navigate when it wasn't critical. She gained confidence and could later cope with long journeys into the unknown.

Boredom and some travel sickness can be kept at bay by staying alert hunting for signposts. Some children find map reading makes them feel ill, and for them a brief list of items to look out for along the route will help them concentrate. They should be encouraged to look out of the front window rather than a side one to reduce car sickness.

Journeys which are to be repeated can have maps embellished with drawings of major landmarks, making it easier for children to recognise each time. They have favourite funny nicknames or jokes that help to remind them what to look for.

• • • • •

walking or cycling

When you're walking or cycling, map reading can be coupled with simple compass reading, and orienteering skills can be developed. On the ground a more intimate relationship is possible with the environment than is the case with car travel, when everything whizzes past. Directions can be on a scale which is more easily understood by a small navigator, so some practice in this is good preparation for a major journey.

identifying

bricknogging

half-timbering

stone

flint and brick

weatherboarding

interesting buildings

A brief guide to building styles can be kept in the car so that travellers can identify styles from a picture easily.

Look for old black and white, oak and plaster. Who can distinguish between genuine and mock?

Look for bricknogging, the zig-zag herringbone effect in red brick.

Look carefully at stonework — is it laid in formal courses, the stones evenly cut, or is it rough with no courses?

Spot the use of flint, often with brick arches.

Some buildings may be tile-hung with the tiles nailed to wooden battens on the exterior walls.

Weatherboarding is where timber boards are fixed one above the other.

Parge (parget or pargetting) is ornamental plaster work used from Tudor times and found in East Anglia and south east England.

Children from about nine years onwards take a lively interest in construction, and can tell the difference between architectural styles and spot distinctive features.

what type of plant or animal is that?

Pocket field guides make spotting flowers, sheep, cattle, trees or birds a fascinating activity. Choose those with very clear illustrations so that children are not frustrated in their search.

• • • • •

origin of place names

Invite children to think about the origins of some of the place names they come across on their holidays and travels. If they were explorers, how would they name a place they had discovered?

This problem faced many early adventurers, such as Captain Cook, Columbus and Vasco da Gama. Occasionally they solved this simply by naming the place after a religious festival occurring when the discovery took place – Easter Island, Ascension Island, Natal (found on Christmas Day). More descriptive names tell of events that happened there on these daring voyages; Cape Runaway and Cape Foulwind suggest some of the problems these intrepid travellers faced. Botany Bay is where Joseph Banks found so many new plants to excite him. And what about Cape Kidnappers, Poverty Bay and Bay of Plenty?

There was also the influence of English Royalty. There were Georges on the throne of England for over 100 years and there are Georgetowns all over the globe. Before the Revolutionary War there was a tendency in America to use names with a royal connection: New York, for example, was named in honour of Charles II's brother, the Duke of York, who later became James II. Many other American place names are derived from Indian words, and can help to teach children about America's Indian heritage. Children can also learn a great deal about the early settlers in America by noting the national origins of city names in various parts of the country. A trip through the American West, for example, may spark a discussion about the early Spanish settlers, while a visit to New Orleans can be a lesson in French language and culture.

I find that children are fascinated by place names and the sense of a living past.

• • • • •

roadsigns

Keep a record of roadsigns seen and look up what they mean.

car games

collect a state

The object of this game is to spot the licence plates from all 50 states. Players keep an eagle eye on the road, looking for new and unfamiliar plates, and recording the state name, the colors and design, and state slogan from each new plate. The player with the most state licence plates listed at the end of the trip wins. Players can then quiz each other on the colors and slogans of each state's plate.

licence plate alphabet

Players study all licence plates, searching for the letters of the alphabet in the correct order. If the letter is out of sequence it cannot be used, but if a licence plate has more than one letter on it in the correct sequence it may be used. With RSY for example, you can score the R and S – provided that you have reached that point in the alphabet and found the Q. You cannot score the Y in the same licence plate.

licence plate bingo

Draw up Bingo cards on paper and, as you see the numbers on a licence plate cross them off on your sheet. The first to complete a sheet wins. This could take some time.

I spotted it first!

It seems nobody has to tell kids how to play this, they do it automatically!

in the
kitchen

let's cook

If you are busy, or work, it is impossible to be a perfect 'Earth Mother', coping smilingly with huge starving broods, with a steaming kitchen filled with homemade loaves and bottled preserves. Those images are bad propaganda. They project an out-of-date concept. They imply that one woman, singlehanded, has done all the preparing and serving of those homemade goodies! Far better to teach these skills to the next generation so that they, too, can produce the goods and don't come to expect one person to wait on them.

Many of us would love to come home to a cosy kitchen with homemade bread and jam at the ready. Well, I often do, but the secret is that I don't do every step of the making myself! Cooking is a rewarding activity for people of all ages because they can enjoy the fruits . . . So, included in this section are some easy, straightforward recipes for family basics.

I am a firm believer in teaching children to cook when very young. One advantage is that they haven't started to say that they don't need your help, and they are willing to learn the right way to do things! It is safer to teach a child to handle a knife with respect rather than forbid its use. No cooking activity should be allowed unless an adult is supervising. Always avoid hot oil with younger cooks, and give them safe jobs to do while you handle the heat and the pouring of hot liquids. When they are teenagers they should be reasonably good, safe, cooks and can be left to produce their own snacks and serve up something tasty for a friend.

Cooking can be absorbing, varied, fun and richly rewarding. A piece of advice to parents of young cooks – have them make only things they like to eat. Results are always better where care and attention are lavished on the dish, and you can't work up an interest in food you're not keen to eat. A freezer makes it possible to cook when you have time and store the result until you need it. So, if it is a dull day and you and the children find the hours hanging heavy, consider a spell in the kitchen making your favourite food.

This is not the place for reams about a healthy diet, but encourage children to take an interest in what their bodies need for health. Do they care enough to see that they eat well? Cooking is just one facet of this preparation for life.

Safety when working with high temperatures and sharp utensils is so important that you will have to impress on your young cooks that they must stick absolutely to certain agreed rules in the kitchen, and **never** work at or use the stove when you are not present.

• • • • •

quick tips

- Making sandwiches is a lot easier with a smooth spread, such as a soft margarine. Butter can be softened slightly by putting a hot bowl upside down over the butter dish. For very young cooks, a flat wooden spatula helps with spreading.

- For snipping chives and parsley, kitchen scissors are easier for small hands than a knife.

- Knife handling can be made easier by winding an elastic band around the handle of the knife to prevent small fingers slipping down towards the blade.

  Make certain that long hair is tied back in a pony tail. It catches in mixers and can burn on stovetop burners.

- Mixing bowls can be made steady by placing a damp kitchen cloth underneath them. This way bowls do not slide around while the child stirs.

- Impress upon your helpers that everything to do with cooking must be spotlessly clean: hands, tools, worktops and cookware.

- An adult should always be nearby if children are in the kitchen.

• • • • •

really easy pea soup   serves 4

To make this soup into a full-scale hearty meal, add slices of tasty cooked sausage. For a velvety texture, try adding a spoonful of yoghurt or thin cream to each bowlful.

    2oz/50g butter
    1 onion, chopped
    1lb/450g frozen peas
    1 pint/600ml chicken stock (or vegetable
        stock for vegetarians)
    salt and freshly ground black pepper
    crisply fried bacon crumbled to garnish
        (optional)

Melt the butter and gently fry the chopped onion for about 5 minutes until it is soft. Add the peas, then add the stock and simmer for 10 minutes. Liquidise the soup and reheat gently. (Your child may use a potato masher to break up the peas and make a thick pulp.) Season to taste. Pour into bowls and sprinkle the bacon bits on the top.

variations

You may use this same method of soup-making with other vegetables. Try 1lb/450g grated carrots with 2 pints (1 litre) stock. Add the carrots to the gently fried onion, as you did with the peas, then add the stock and simmer for about 20 minutes until the carrots are soft. Season with a little ground coriander and a sprinkle of mace. Liquidise, or mash, and season with salt and freshly ground black pepper plus one level teaspoon of sugar. (Substitute nutmeg for mace if required.)

• • • • •

the easiest bread

Making your own bread is easier than you think. Kneading it is as much fun for children as kneading and rolling clay, but there is a much better result. The warm fragrant yeasty smell of the baking bread – and the taste of it fresh from the oven –are worth the cleaning up!

There is a type of dried yeast, known as "fast acting" which is available in little sachets. This requires no first stage of frothing with water and sugar. It makes the recipe that follows both quick and easy.

1½lb/675g wholemeal flour
2 teaspoons salt
1oz/25g lard, cut in pieces
1 sachet fast acting yeast
¾ pint/450ml warm water
sesame seeds

Turn the oven on to heat (Gas 6/425°F/220°C) at the start and the warm kitchen will help the process. The flour should be at room temperature or a little warm.

Mix flour and salt. Rub in the lard with fingertips. Open the yeast sachet and sprinkle the granules on the flour. Stir to blend evenly. Make a well in the centre of the flour and add the warm water all at once. Stir firmly and try to draw in as

much of the loose flour as you can. You will soon have a large mass of dough. If it seems too wet, sprinkle on a little flour; if too hard and heavy, add a few drops of water. The dough should be kneaded with the heel of the hand in a warm place for 10 minutes. It should feel elastic and hold its shape.

Let children take turns to punch it down and knead it again and again during this stage.

Grease a 2 lb pan with lard and sprinkle some of the sesame seeds into it. Shape the dough into a fat sausage shape and put it into the pan. Sprinkle more of the sesame seeds over the top of the loaf. If they don't stick, sprinkle a few drops of water over it to act as glue.

Cover the loaf with a clean tea towel soaked in hot water and squeezed out. Leave in a warm place to rise for about 30 minutes. Carefully remove the cloth and bake at Gas 6/425°F/220°C in the pre-heated oven for 30 minutes. The bread is done when it sounds hollow when tapped underneath. Take it out of the pan and stand on a cooling rack until cool. Cut when cool.

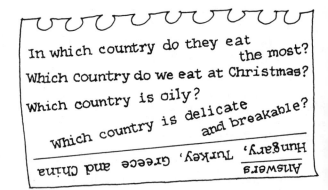

In which country do they eat the most?
Which country do we eat at Christmas?
Which country is oily?
Which country is delicate and breakable?

Answers
Hungary, Turkey, Greece and China

the easiest pizza

Pizza has many interesting and easy stages in its preparation. Cooks of varying ages should be able to enjoy some of the work, and all enjoy choosing their fillings and sprinkling them on. Pizzas were traditionally baked in a specially built brick oven, on a flat wooden shovel. They need such a very high heat that adult help is essential for this stage. Eat straight from the oven.

I have used tea cups for measuring as this is far easier for children. (You may substitute a packet of white bread mix for the base.) For one large 10"/25cm pizza (to feed four if a slice is all that is needed, two for a main course) or four small 4"/10cm pizzas you will need:

> 1½ cups strong plain flour (sifted)
> salt
> ⅓ sachet Dried Active Yeast
> 2 tablespoons oil
> ½ cup warm water

Tip the flour into a large bowl with a pinch of salt and the yeast granules. Add 2 tablespoons of oil. Add ½ cup hand-hot water and mix all together to form a soft pliable dough. If it is too sticky, sprinkle lightly with flour. Knead well by hand for 10 minutes. Children can each do a lump if they are making small individual ones.

The dough should become smooth and elastic. Put it to rise in an oiled bowl, cover with a damp, clean cloth and leave in a warm place for 30 minutes for the dough to rise.

Preheat the oven to Gas 7/450°F/230°C and prepare the topping during this time.

filling

Most pizzas begin with a *passato*. This is a thick tomato sauce made from tomatoes, canned or fresh, but not ketchup or purée. It can be bought ready in cartons and cans in supermarkets. Alternatively use a can of chopped plum tomatoes.

Prepare a selection of favourite ingredients: grated mozzarella cheese, anchovies, stoned black olives, chopped green pepper, chopped mushrooms, chopped ham or any other tastes you like. Fry the mushrooms for a moment or two in a little olive oil and set aside. Have ready olive oil, oregano, pepper and salt.

When the dough is risen, punch it down and knead and flatten into a thin circle about 10"/25cm in diameter, or into four small 4"/10cm circles, and fit into a pizza pan, or lay on a baking sheet.

Spread the tomato base all over the dough. Have each child choose his or her favourite toppings, and add them along with generous sprinklings of grated mozzarella. Drizzle a little olive oil over the whole thing and sprinkle with oregano, a little black pepper and a tiny sprinkle of salt. Top with extra cheese and bake for approximately 15 minutes until the cheese is melted and bubbling. Pizza burns quickly at this heat so keep alert.

· · · · ·

hamburger

Assemble the perfect hamburger of your choice! Most children (and adults) have their own particular idea of hamburger perfection. Some like gherkins, others loathe them, and so it goes with all the possible garnishes. Let your child assemble his or her own from the various possibilities. Hamburger parties work well on this principle too.

Experiment with layers of bun (gently warmed), tomato sauce, gherkins, onions, lettuce, tomato, cheese, pink sauce (tomato and mayonnaise), plus of course the burger itself, a quarter of a pound (100g) of beef. If you are a vegetarian, a gourmet delight can be made with a soya burger. An adult or an older child can grill the burgers and the younger ones can assemble them.

· · · · ·

homemade peanut butter

Use fresh roasted peanuts or salted peanuts. In a blender or food processor, grind the nuts with a little vegetable oil if it seems dry (1½ tablespoons per cup of nuts) and add salt if the nuts are not already salted (½ teaspoon salt per cup of nuts). This is a nourishing spread to lavish on a slice of your own homemade bread.

the easiest cake

Making a cake using the method known as 'all in one' simply means that you put all the ingredients into a bowl and beat them. This is quick and easy and cuts out many of the traditional steps in cake making. For young cooks it is fast and direct.

> 8oz/225g granulated sugar
> 4 large eggs
> 4 tablespoons milk
> grated orange rind (a zester is a neat little gadget that rasps the rind off)
> 8oz/225g soft margarine
> 12oz/350g self-rising flour

Preheat the oven to Gas 4/350°F/180°C. Grease and flour two 8"/20cm pans. You do this by smearing the butter or margarine around the base and sides of the pans with a little greaseproof paper. Even the youngest helper can do this. Make certain that every part of the surface is covered. Tip a tablespoon of flour into each pan and then tilt the pan so that the flour is sprinkled all over the base and sides. Flour will stick to the grease; surplus flour will come loose if you gently tap the pan with your fingers rotating it so that flour coming loose can attach itself elsewhere.

Put all the ingredients into a large bowl. With a big wooden spoon a child can stir the ingredients together to form a sticky mixture. Gather in the dry flour, then pour the mixture evenly into the two pans.

Bake for 40 minutes, or until the cakes have shrunk away at the edges and spring back when you press the centre gently with a fingertip. Cool on a rack. Sandwich together when cool with jam or icing.

• • • • •

easy oatmeal scones

Quick, easy and wholesome, these delicious scones need little equipment or handling. If you have no scone cutter, use an upturned glass to cut out the circles. Again, I have used tea cups for quick measuring.

> 1½ cups plain flour
> 1 teaspoon baking soda
> 2 teaspoons cream of tartar
> ¼ teaspoon salt
> 2 tablespoons soft butter
> ⅔ cup rolled oats
> ½ cup milk
> 1 egg yolk
> 1 teaspoon water } for glaze

Preheat the oven to Gas 7/425°F/220°C.

Sift the flour, baking soda, cream of tartar and salt into a large mixing bowl. Rub in the butter and oats with your fingertips. Stir in the milk and form a soft pliable dough.

Knead lightly with your hands on a floured board. Pat the dough down lightly until it is 1½"/4cm thick. Do not flatten it roughly. Cut out rounds with a scone cutter and place them on a greased baking sheet.

Mix the egg yolk and the water and brush the tops of your scones with this glaze. Bake for 10 minutes.

Makes approximately 12 scones

• • • • •

make your own popsicles

For these homemade popsicles you need a carton of concentrated fruit juice, or freshly squeezed juice, an ice cube tray and either some wooden popsicle sticks which the kids have collected and washed, or the little wooden spoons that come with tub ice creams.

To make, simply pour the juice into an ice cube tray and put into the freezer. When the juice is almost frozen, mushy and thick, put in your wooden handles, standing them carefully upright. Leave the popsicles to freeze solid.

homemade ice cream

This is the most delicious ice cream ever. Vary the flavour as you wish: rum-and-raisin would take a few drops of rum flavouring and some finely chopped up raisins; chocolate chips and pieces of flake may be mixed in . . . Use your imagination – and let your child do the beating.

    4 egg yolks
    6 fl oz/170ml sweetened condensed milk
    2½ cups/700ml double cream (1¼ pints)
    1 teaspoon vanilla extract (or other
       flavouring)
    4 egg whites

Beat the egg yolks and the condensed milk until thick, creamy and fluffy. Beat the cream until thick but not dry, and add to the egg/milk mixture. Add your chosen flavouring.

Beat up the egg whites until stiff. Fold them into the egg/cream mixture with a metal spoon using a light cutting action. Place in a container in the freezer. When almost set, take out and beat well once more to break up the ice crystals. Replace in the freezer until no one can resist it any longer.

• • • • •

lemon and barley water

A refreshing drink. To be made by an adult *for* children. While you make it, a child can design a label for the bottle.

    4oz/100g pearl barley
    grated rind and squeezed juice of 2 lemons
    2oz/50g sugar
    4 cups boiling water

Wash the barley. Put it in a large saucepan and cover it with cold water. Bring to the boil and boil for 4 minutes, then strain.

Put the barley into a large heat-proof jug with the grated lemon rind and the sugar. Pour the 4 cups of boiling water over the barley and stir until the sugar has dissolved. Leave it to cool, then add the lemon juice. Chill until cold.

This drink may be diluted to taste with iced water or mineral water.

• • • • •

crystallised flowers

This is a luxurious and glamorous decoration to a table (if you crystallise a rose) or to a dish (if you use violets).

Wash and carefully dry the flowers. If rose petals come apart, do not worry as they can be reassembled. Whip an egg white to soft peaks and, using a clean paintbrush, cover the petals with this. Leave no bald spots. Dip any loose petals into the egg white. When the flower is completely coated dip it into granulated sugar. This can also be dredged all over the flower. (Place the flower on greaseproof paper for this and reuse the sugar which falls on to the paper.) Arrange them on greaseproof paper on baking trays.

Leave the flowers to dry in a very slow oven, barely on, or in an airing cupboard. They will become crystallised in about 1½–2 hours. You can gently reassemble loose petals now with the aid of the paintbrush dipped into the sticky egg white.

• • • • •

chocolate leaves

You may want to add beautiful glossy chocolate leaves to your snowy flower. The leaves that work best are waxy, shiny leaves rather than the furry sort.

Melt dark chocolate in a bowl over a basin of hot water. Coat the underside of the washed leaves with the chocolate and leave them in the fridge to harden. Peel off carefully and use.

the kitchen factory

There are many things to make in the kitchen, not all of them for eating. This is the place that can be a laboratory, an art room and a production plant. Surfaces are, or should be, easy to clean up. Water is on hand, and there is a wide variety of fascinating tools.

how is butter made?

If you would like to spread homemade butter on a slice of The Easiest Bread, and your children are feeling restless, let them use their pent-up energy making it!

In a jar with a tight fitting lid place some double cream and some *clean* glass marbles. Have them shake it up and down and generally agitate it steadily. Butter will form. Strain through muslin or cheesecloth, rinse the butter and taste.

School dinners, school dinners,
Mushy peas, mushy peas,
Soggy semolina, soggy semolina,
I feel sick,
Bring a bucket quick.
It's too late,
I did it on my plate.
I've done more
on the floor.

Clap or skip; sung to the tune of Frère Jacques.

herb vinegar

Make your own flavoured vinegars with fresh herbs.

Have your helpers pick fresh young leaves off sprigs of mint, thyme, basil, marjoram or tarragon. Wash them, then place in bottles and pour in good vinegar (use approximately 3 tablespoons of herbs to around 4 cups of vinegar). Seal tightly and let steep for about four weeks. The vinegar will take on the flavour of the herbs. Strain and re-bottle leaving only one sprig of the herbs inside. Now design a label for your family vinegar.

fragrant soap balls

These are made from leftover soap scraps. The makers will first need to collect around 7oz/200g of scraps.

Grate or chop up the scraps and place them in a large bowl. Pour over ¼ teacup heated rose-water and allow this mixture to set for 10–15 minutes, then mix it well.

Beat in a few drops of lavender oil, a drop at a time using a blender on slow speed. (Adult super-vision needed for all appliances.) Leave it to cool. Pour into a small round bowl. Do not handle or disturb for three days.

When the soap has begun to dry out and harden, roll it into little balls between the palms of your hands. They should dry out further in the sun or in a warm place. Finally, to give them a sheen, dampen your hands with rosewater and roll the balls once more in your hands for a smooth finish. Arrange these soap balls in small baskets or large flat sea shells. They make charming old-fashioned gifts.

make your own bubble mixture

In a bowl, mix 1 cup dishwashing liquid with 2 cups warm water and 3 tablespoons glycerine. Add ½ teaspoon of sugar.

Dishwashing liquids vary in their concentration, but most work well. Glycerine is added to give the bubbles lasting power, but may be left out if you cannot get it. (Chemists stock it.)

Blow your bubbles through either a wire twisted into rings, or through a drinking straw, or through a bunch of straws for multiple bubbles. For a larger size bubble, use a paper cup: punch a hole in the base of the cup, dip the rim into the bubble mix and then gently blow through the hole that you punched.

Bubbles sting eyes if they pop too close. If you have a child who is sensitive about this, let them wear swimming goggles or sunglasses.

the kitchen laboratory

The kitchen is also a laboratory where your family can observe and experiment. Maths becomes a reality as you examine objects and weigh them or measure them. Are all large objects heavier than smaller ones? Entertain six and seven-year-olds with weighing experiments. Then try measuring how much water various containers will hold. At first glance it may look as though one is bigger than another, but when the water it contains is measured they may find that this is not so.

Small children use words such as 'bigger' or 'smaller' at first, and the kitchen is the easiest place in which to learn concepts such as heavy or light, wide or narrow, deep or shallow as you look at cups, saucers, cuboid cereal packets and paper towel inner tubes.

a few experiments

Did you know that there is air in water?
Fill a glass with water and stand it on a sunny windowsill. As the air is warmed, bubbles expand, gather on the inside of the glass and escape.

Did you know that temperature affects touch?
Your child holds two fingers on an ice cube until they feel numb and frozen. Then she touches various objects around her. What can she feel?

Did you know that warm water rises?
Take two milk bottles. Fill each with water, one hot and the other cold. Dye the water in the hot one with food colouring or ink. Place a piece of card over the top of the one holding cold water. (This is the adult's job: holding the card firmly, tip the cold bottle upside down and place it on top of the neck of the bottle of hot water, sliding out the card smoothly. Best done in the sink.)

Now everyone watches as the coloured water rises, swirling up through the cold water.

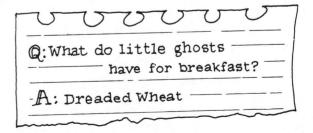

Q: What do little ghosts have for breakfast?

A: Dreaded Wheat

Do you want to make water run uphill?

Collect two empty jars and a drinking straw made of plastic with a concertina bend in it. (These are available at most supermarkets.) Fill one of the jars with water. Put this filled jar on the draining board close to the edge of the sink. Put the empty jar in the sink, as close as you can to the first jar.

Look closely at your straw. The bend is closer to one end, and I shall call this the short end. Put this short end into the jar with the water and hold it under the water level. Put the other end into your mouth and gently suck up some water. When you take your mouth away the water will continue to run *UP* the straw to the bend and then down the length of the straw into your empty jar in the sink.

Why do corks always float lying in one direction?

There are little air pockets in cork called lenticels and they lie in one direction. Corks for bottles must be cut at right angles to the lenticels, otherwise air would get through the cork into the wine in the bottle. By cutting the corks in this way they form a seal. Whichever way you turn your cork while it floats in water, it will turn itself around and come back to the same direction.

See also the Magic Cork trick, page 92.

Can you still taste when your nose is smelling something else?

Blindfold a child. Put a piece of fruit into his mouth while holding a slice of onion near his nose. Can he tell what the fruit is?

Look at sponges

While washing up or in the bath, take a closer look at a sponge with a child. Feel how the sponge is light when dry and heavier when it has soaked up water. A small child will be fascinated to try some of this sponge play. Ask questions such as, 'Where has the water gone to?' after soaking up a puddle with a dry sponge. Squeeze out the sponge and measure the water together in a measuring jug. You might like to weigh your sponge before and after for another way of measuring how much water it sucks up. Does a natural sponge suck up more than a foam sponge of the same size? What happens to the air in the sponge?

plant life in the kitchen

A casual visitor to our home might wonder why we have given so much space to plants when there is so little of it in our tiny kitchen. A quick trip to the fridge and a child must negotiate the fronds and foliage. She cannot fail to notice them. This is the point! In any other room the plants are seen occasionally, but in the kitchen we see them umpteen times a day, noticing any changes in their growth and flowering.

The kitchen is full of opportunities to grow plants from food we eat. Pips, seeds, carrot tops and sprouts are here in abundance. We can also grow food that we will eat next week!

On the kitchen windowsill I grow pots of herbs: swordlike chives for snipping, rosemary and thyme. This is the place where we keep all our cuttings in glass jars, so that we can inspect them often and monitor the growth of those amazing roots. Impatient young farmers grow and harvest a crop of cress within four days.

It is in the warmth of our kitchen that a stem of pussywillow will open into spectacular silken

silver fluff faster than it would in any other room. A willow wand taken in spring and stood in a glass jar will quickly produce the palest, juiciest green leaves and, because the family will be in the kitchen so often, these changes and miracles will be noticed.

This pleasure, this huge reward, is ours for very little effort. Our avocado pip vigorously swells and puts forth roots, balanced precariously on its toothpick arms in a glass of water. Our cress thrives and is eaten. The weeping fig is too tall for the room, but is obligingly growing along the ceiling. We can barely see out of that window, and the view does not merit a look! But the plants inside that window . . . they have truly expanded the horizon of this narrow room, and, on a cooped-up day, one could imagine oneself in a far off jungle.

there is life in dried up seeds

With patience, you can sprout dried peas, apple pips or even hamster seed mix! Some will take longer than others. An acorn, though slow, is spectacular: wrap it in damp cottonwool and put into a plastic bag. Gather a few seeds on a walk and try to germinate them. Scrape the mud from your child's boots after a walk in a field and mix with a little potting compost. A wide variety of plants will grow and show him or her how cleverly plants distribute their seeds.

• • • • •

prepare for spring

Dull day? Wintry weather? Prepare for spring by planting seeds so that they get a warm headstart indoors. This is a group activity, ideal for workers of different ages.

● Use yoghurt pots or ice cream containers. Wash these out thoroughly and punch holes in the bases.

● Fill with a fine sandy potting mix or compost mixed with a little river sand. To make it fine enough, sift it a couple of times first.

- Fill the pot loosely. Give it a sharp knock so that the soil drops down a little.

- Place the seeds on top of the soil.

- Cover with river sand to a depth of twice the thickness of the seed. Very fine seeds will have to sit on top of the soil.

- Gently firm the sand down level with a spoon or with the base of another pot. Water lightly.

- Label your seed with name and date.

- Put in a safe spot away from direct sunlight and draughts.

- To make seeds germinate quicker, cover with a sheet of card to start them off.

- Keep seeds at an even temperature.

- Check to see that they don't dry out.

- If you have to leave your seeds unattended for several days, place the pot on a few pebbles in a larger one, and fill the outer pot with 1"/2.5cm water.

- When the seeds have germinated, water only from above. Remove the outer container if you have used one.

- Replant your seeds while they are still small into bigger pots.

Even the best gardeners have some failures with seeds, so plant more than you think you'll need.

• • • • •

see growth at first hand

Line a glass tumbler with blotting paper and put some water in the glass. Place sunflower seeds, corn or beans between the paper and the glass and you will be rewarded with a perfect view as they sprout and grow. Check regularly to maintain the water level at the bottom of your glass. This should not dry up. Keep this growing glass in a light spot, but out of the direct sun. The miracle of growth seen close-up will be enjoyed by children if the glass is near a breakfast table or another spot they come to often.

• • • • •

a little lawn

Cover a moist sponge with grass seed. Place in a saucer of water in a bright window. Keep it moist and in a few days you will have a mini lawn.

water guzzlers

Mark the water level in a glass jar into which you have put a stem of Impatiens. Watch together how quickly the plant drinks the water. On subsequent days mark the level of the water again.

printing with plants

Printing with leaves and vegetables gives an instant diagram, illustrating how they are constructed.

Paint the underside of a leaf and press it on to a clean sheet of paper. The paint should not be too wet. Gently lift off your leaf and you will be able to see the veins and shape of the leaf clearly outlined. Slice a floret of cauliflower across and take a print from this; try an onion for spectacular results showing all the layers; and see how cleverly mushrooms are built.

Read more about printing on page 72.

mini gardens

Create a miniature landscape in its own climate by making a garden in a bottle. For this you will need a large glass container. Place some charcoal in the bottom of the bottle, then with a paper funnel to help you get it safely in, pour a fine layer of gravel into it to form a drainage layer. Using the funnel again, pour in the soil. Use a mixture of potting compost and river sand. Press the soil down evenly with a tool made from sticking a cork on to the end of a knitting needle. Chopsticks, if your child can handle them, are helpful in the planting work.

Slow growing and attractive plants that enjoy a humid atmosphere are the most suitable for your glass garden. Children will need help in the selection of plants. Once they are established they will need very little attention. Water that evaporates from the leaves will condense on the glass and trickle down again to the roots. Check to see that the soil does not eventually dry out due to heating or sunlight, and also check that it is not too wet.

Tinier gardens still can be made in other containers. Cress can be grown in an empty egg shell lined with kitchen towel, a violet can be grown prettily in a wine glass or an old china teacup. As these two don't have drainage holes a sandy soil with a little charcoal will be necessary.

On a larger scale, mini gardens may be planted in old sinks or troughs. Trays that are not too shallow might be suitable if you built up some little mounds or hills. Let children landscape this; perhaps a meandering path might be built with fine gravel. Drop a container with water in it down into the soil to make a tiny pond. There are miniature roses, ferns and mosses that will be the right size for a mini garden.

This is peaceful work, moulding the landscape to some personal plan, and imagining what goes on within it. It might be on another planet, or a secret garden, a farm or cattle ranch.

pressed flowers to capture summer

Kids love collecting flowers to press. Make a sandwich of these between two sheets of blotting paper or kitchen towel. Put this between the pages of some old telephone books or other heavy volumes. The flowers must form one layer only; if they lie on top of one another they will not dry well. Pile up a few more heavy objects on top of the books and leave undisturbed for at least three weeks.

When you take them out, the flowers will be quite flat and can be made into artistic designs and pictures to stick on to card as bookmarks. Cover this with acetate or adhesive sheet. When you need to fix the petals in position, use egg white as it will dry transparent.

• • • • •

a few suggestions

- Experiment with growing plants in the dark and in the light to prove that plants need light.

- Watch how seedlings will lean over towards the sunny window. What happens if you turn the pot around the other way?

- Make a fragrant pot-pourri to perfume your home. Layer dried rose petals with common salt. Add dried orange peel, crushed cloves, orris powder and a drop of essential oil. Leave to steep, covered and sealed, for six weeks.

- Thread up seeds for an unusual necklace.

- Hang bunches of flowers upside down to dry. Tie with elastic bands to allow for shrinkage.

- Grow a hyacinth in a glass of water.

- Grow carrot or pineapple tops in a saucer of water on a windowsill.

- Show your children potatoes and radishes sprouting if left too long in the kitchen.

- Sprout sunflower seeds, alfalfa, peas, lentils, soya beans and wheat in a saucer with damp cotton.

- Take cuttings in various ways. Stem cuttings and leaf cuttings are fascinating to watch as they grow into replicas of their parents.

- Grow corn and butter beans in a saucer so you can compare single and double leafed shoots.

- Books of old herbal remedies abound; make up one or two recipes and see if they work!

- Boiled plants yield dyes in soft natural shades. Check a library for information on how to use these.

in a
creative mood

It's a good feeling to stand back, look at your handiwork and know that you made it yourself. Grouped here are suggestions which will give pleasure in the making and yield a tangible result.

Satisfying in so many ways, creative craftwork and art techniques are pastimes that know no age limits; design plays an important part in the lives of everyone. Here is a chance for a child to re-think the layout of his or her room, or consider a design for an object used every day, or even create a strip cartoon character.

Mastering new techniques may unlock skills and talent children have not yet tapped. Simply showing them a way with a new material, or a different method of applying the paint, can set off new trains of thought and stimulate them to experiment. Like bubbles in a bottle of champagne, children's ideas come bursting out when you pull the cork by creating the opportunities.

One area of visual interest is the optical illusion, which leads us to consider other illusions around us in architecture and in items as commonplace as picture frames. Get kids started and they will spot them everywhere.

Drawing can also take a purely practical form as in map or plan drawing. Designs and working drawings for something we intend to construct allow us to correct mistakes and test ideas on paper before committing them to their final form. This is useful for planning a new layout for a bedroom, before heaving the furniture around, and for something as delicate as a model of a plane.

All around us are visual images. Advertising and signposts are two of the many ways we receive messages. Children are generally very aware of advertising, and enjoy trying their hand at it. Spend a while designing a poster and you suddenly become aware of every poster in the street, in the underground or on a tatty old wall! Creative effort expands our consciousness and makes us less likely to tolerate the ugly. Each generation influences the environment through taste and design changes, looking at everything with a fresh eye.

With my own children I have spent many hours considering design as it relates to architecture, interior design, and, of course clothes. 'What's happened to your taste, mom?' is a line I hear often. The pupil soon overtakes the teacher and the child becomes critical of the parent!

paper folding

Paper folding is an art performed with no tools save your hands. The paper is folded and creased to form sculptures of purity and originality. Some accuracy is needed, so this is not suitable for under sevens without help.

pop-up card

Pop-up cards are easier to make than you might think. Children love the element of surprise and will enjoy giving them to family and friends. Try this method of folding a sheet of paper to make a card with an internal pop-up section which can be decorated.

You will need a sheet of paper that is fairly stiff. It must be a rectangle. Place the sheet vertically and follow the diagrams.

1 Place the sheet on a table with the short side towards you. Fold in half down the centre, left edge towards right edge. The fold is on your left.

2 Now take the top left hand corner and fold it down to meet and line up with the right hand edges.

3 Open out again, also opening out your original fold.

4 With the paper flat in its original position, fold the lower edge up to the top edge and crease the centre fold.

5 Turn the whole card over. Fold it in half from left to right.

6 Encourage the centre top edge of your inner layer to bend forward reversing the creases you made in step 2. Now you have a card with an inner layer which pops forward.

7 With a pair of scissors carefully cut across all the layers ⅓ the way down.

8 When the card is opened, the inner section pops up over the outer edge. If you wish, you may add paper shapes to the pop-up section, taking care, though, that they remain hidden when the card is closed. On an owl, for example, add feathers and a beak. Decorate.

Pop-up card

1. fold in half

2. fold down top left corner and line up edges

3. open out

4. crease fold

take bottom edge up to top edge, fold in half

5. turn whole card over and fold in half from left to right

6. encourage inner V-shaped fold to bend forward on the creases

7. ⅓

cut across all layers, ⅓ from top edge

8. this area pops up

decorate your card; write message

origami – jumping frog

Many amazing playthings can be created from a piece of square paper using traditional Japanese origami techniques. Paper folding is a precise and accurate art needing patience and skill, yet masterpieces can be made very simply with practice. Begin with an easy design such as this jumping frog, and if your paper folding group would like to try some more complicated shapes there are many books containing these in libraries.

Origami paper can be found in craft shops and many stationers and bookshops. Good results are possible with a wide range of papers: all you need is a perfect square and preferably paper with some body to it. Writing paper is usually heavy enough. You could use green paper for a more froglike appearance.

1 Fold opposite edges together in turn, crease each fold and then open. First bottom edge to top edge, then left edge to right edge.

2 With fold open, make new folds: take each corner to the centre. Crease folds.

3 It is now diamond shaped. Fold top two edges to centre line. Crease folds.

4 With pointed end at the top, fold up lower triangle.

5 Fold each lower corner into the centre of the lower edge.

6 Now fold lower edge upward.

7 Fold top half of rectangle down.

8 Make a 'head' by folding the point downward.

9 Turn over.

10 Apply pressure on the frog's back with your forefinger, sliding your finger backwards down the model. The little frog will jump forward away from your finger.

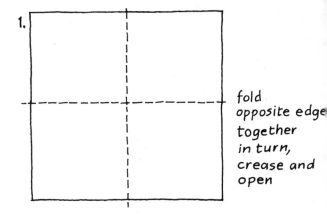

1. fold opposite edge together in turn, crease and open

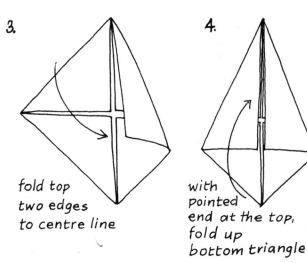

3. fold top two edges to centre line

4. with pointed end at the top, fold up bottom triangle

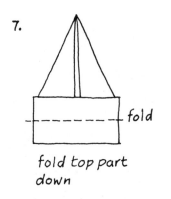

7. fold top part down

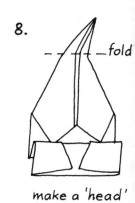

8. fold

make a 'head'

2.

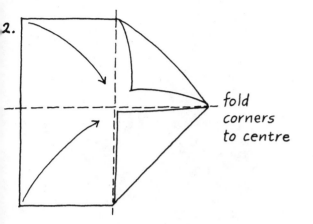

fold corners to centre

Here are some ideas to set you off experimenting with folded paper. Show children one or two at first, and let them experiment and discover.

• • • • •

symmetrical designs with folded paper

Symmetrical means a design that is exactly the same on each side of a middle line. This could be an imaginary line in your design, or, much easier, the fold in your piece of paper.

cut along the fold

Fold a piece of paper in half and make a series of cuts along the fold, cutting away notches and triangles of paper. Open out the paper sheet and lay it on a sheet of contrasting colour.

5.

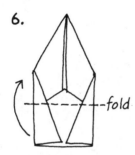

fold each bottom corner into the centre of the lower edge

6.

—fold

fold lower edge upward

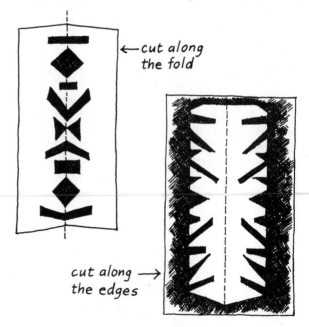

←cut along the fold

cut along → the edges

turn over . . .

press finger down and slide back – your frog will now jump!

cut along the edges

Now try another one in which you make your cuts on the edges of the folded sheet, rather than on the fold. This gives a different effect.

fold again

Next try folding the paper into four – and later eight – thicknesses and cutting patterns into all the layers. When you open the paper out, exciting and dramatic patterns will appear.

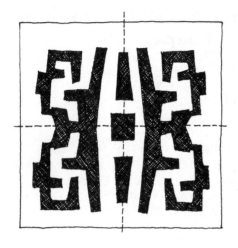

ink blob patterns

Folding paper can produce another type of symmetrical pattern. Drop a blob of ink on to the paper, then fold carefully, and gently open. A perfectly symmetrical pattern will have formed on the page. Experiment with this and try to make the paint shapes more distinct by painting them on before folding the paper. This will give a clearer more defined design than the blob method. Try white paint on black paper.

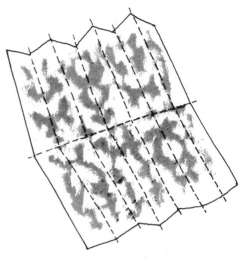

pleating

Folds become more intricate once you have learnt how to make ink blob patterns. From your first simple fold (sheet folded in half), branch out and try folding vertically in lots of little pleats, then fold in half two or three times. As you make each fold, press the paint away with your fingers. Finally, when you carefully open it out, you will have a repeated 'blob' pattern.

fold and dip

If you like doing intricate folding, prepare the paper first by folding it as many times as you like, then try dipping corners of it into the ink or paint. When this is opened out you will see very exciting shapes.

To block off some areas, pinch the folds closed with a clothes peg or bulldog clip. The paint will not be able to reach these folds. In this way the design will have coloured areas and blank ones in a symmetrical or repeated pattern according to the folds. Accordion pleats, fan shapes, and combinations of these with centre folds, work well with paper that is not too thick. Try greaseproof paper from the kitchen, with fountain pen ink for dipping, or rice paper and food colouring.

what can you do with a cardboard carton?

Children as young as seven will take over the project with enthusiasm once you have helped them begin. Their imagination can run riot as they carpet, wallpaper and generally 'furnish' this doll's house. The fort is very quickly made and then forms the basis of many games. Soon they will see ideas in cartons, and papers and dream up other structures to make. If you buy a new washing machine they will take over the box and create a dwelling of their own.

doll's house

You will need:

an empty carton (the sort supermarkets receive their goods in)

a sheet of flat cardboard 2"/5cm longer than the length E–F of your carton (see diagram), and at least the same width. Call this rectangle A

a second rectangle of card, rectangle B. The height is the same as C–D of your carton, but the width is 1"/2.5cm narrower than D–E

The detailed, difficult work on your house should be done while the pieces are separate. Once assembled, you should need only to arrange the furniture and the people who will live in it.

1 Trim these pieces of cardboard neatly and check that corners are square.

2 Now cut the slot, as marked on the diagram, through the centre of rectangle A, almost to the end. Stop 1"/2.5cm before the edge.

3 Cut slots, as shown, in the sides of your carton, also stopping before the end is reached.

4 Piece B is to become the vertical dividing wall and will be seen in four different rooms. Stick remnants of wallpaper or giftwrap on to the four walls to suit your colour schemes.

5 Rectangle A will be the floor of the upstairs rooms which will need to be 'carpeted', tiled, or even given a parquet wood look with one of the doll's house papers available. The underside of this will form ceilings in the lower rooms. These can be simply painted, or elaborately decorated with drawings of mouldings and light fittings.

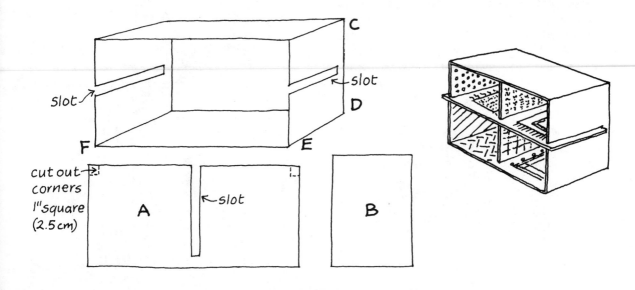

6 Decide where you would like to have windows or even a skylight. Before cutting out spaces for these, look for suitable pieces of transparent plastic, and then cut holes to fit your finds. Use plastic covers from 'bubble' packs of cosmetics and toiletries. These are a good shape and protrude from the house rather like bay windows, giving depth for a sill. A skylight can give much needed light which will fall directly from above, making it easier to play with this house at night.

7 Curtains are made by pleating scraps of fabric and glueing them on the window. Curtains could be hung on rails made from toothpicks or cocktail sticks and little rings of metal often found in bead threading kits.

8 Finally slot piece B into the slot on A, and then gently slide them into the slots you made in your carton.

People can be made for the house or fort from pipe cleaners, twisted to form the body and limbs. Small garments simply tacked together transform these wire frames into expressive people. Hair is made from wool scraps, or for a white-haired granny, cotton. Fuse wire is bent to form a pair of glasses.

The garden and driveway of the house can be landscaped on a piece of scrap masonite. A luscious lawn was ours for a few cents when we bought the artificial green grass used at a local fruit stall. Paint grey pavement, cobble with lentils, or use sandpaper as gravel for the driveway.

Remember to think carefully about scale. The size of one article must be roughly right in relation to others. Furniture can be made from matchboxes; they can be glued together in 'chest of drawers' combinations, upholstered with slivers of foam and some fabric, or used to build a staircase.

fort

A fort can be made by using cardboard tubes from kitchen towel packs for the corner towers. Fit these on to the corners of a cardboard carton and add little cardboard cones on the top of each tube. Cut out doorways and make battlements on the top of the carton. This crenellated edge is a good design for soldiers to shield behind and fire from.

A second carton, a little smaller than the first, can be placed inside the fort, upside down. This gives the soldiers a platform to stand on near the battlements, and double thick walls to protect them from the enemy when they are inside the fort. Cut the doors through both cartons at carefully aligned positions.

This fort can stand on a piece of masonite with a sandpaper substitute for gravel. Simply glue a sheet of sandpaper on to the board wherever you want a gravel look. Use the coarsest grade you can find. Lentils glued down will look like cobblestones. Paint the outside of your fort with a stone pattern. Make flags to fly on toothpicks or matchsticks. Instead of windows, some forts had small slits through which soldiers could take aim, or keep watch.

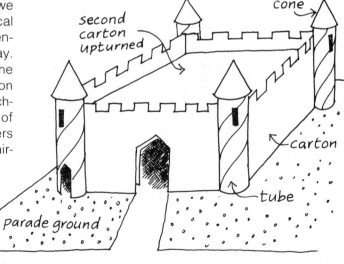

learn new methods

marbling

The swirling varied delicate patterns of marbled papers have always held a special appeal for me. A look at the flyleaf (end papers) of an old book will show any would-be marbler what to aim for.

This technique works because oil and water don't mix.

You will need:

1 oil paint or oil-based inks
2 a tray or shallow dish filled with water
3 vinegar or dishwashing liquid
4 paper
5 a large area covered with newspaper

Carefully drip some paint or ink colours on to the surface of the water. A few drops of vinegar help to break up and disperse the oil colours: alternatively, a few drops of dishwashing liquid will stir the paint into action. Lay a sheet of paper carefully on to the water. It will absorb the paint. Gently lift off and lay to dry on the newspaper.

Experiment by pouring, dripping or spraying the oil-based paint on to the water. Each method will give a different result.

If you do not have any oil-based paint or ink to hand, you could try this technique with ordinary ink on water. However, this will give you only one marbled print as the ink will soon sink down into the water. Carefully draw the sheet of paper over the surface of the water holding the two corners. Act quickly as there is only a short period before the ink sinks!

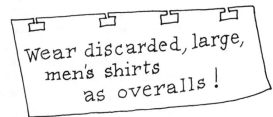

Wear discarded, large, men's shirts as overalls!

wet-on wet

Paint or ink reacts when it is put on to a wet surface, spreading and staining into patterns of its own. Try dropping splats of paint or ink on to a previously wetted surface and watch how the spots behave. Ink, indian ink, watercolour or poster paints can be tried out on different sorts of paper: newsprint, shiny, smooth, cartridge paper, absorbent paper towels, even ordinary grease-proof paper. Try wetting some areas of the paper with wet cotton, then drip on the ink. Ink will spread more easily with a drop of washing up liquid added to it.

Another experiment is to drip ink on to absorbent paper such as blotting paper. This can be tried with wet and dry paper, and with diluted ink.

To keep greater control of a staining pattern, paint a design on to the page in clean water, then drip a little ink on to the wet areas with the wooden tip of the brush handle.

Experiment with watercolours (a) by painting on to a damp surface, and (b) by painting directly on to the paper and then holding the paper under running water. This will give an effect called a wash and there will be a soft coloured tint on your paper.

· · · · ·

resisting the colour with wax

On plain lining paper, draw with wax crayons and then put a one colour watercolour wash over the whole sheet. The colour cannot penetrate the wax, so the areas painted with wax will not take up the watercolour tint. When the first wash is dry, you can draw once more with wax and do a second wash. Where the second wax drawing has gone over the first colour it will protect it and stop the second colour covering this part of the design. In this way a design with several colours is gradually built up. If you plan to use several colours, start with the lightest one first and gradually build towards the darkest with each wash.

The wax can be removed by putting the picture between thick layers of newspaper and ironing it with a warm iron until the wax melts and is absorbed by the newspaper. This is a job for an adult.

As with all these techniques, if you work with young artists the first time to show how it is done, or to discover this for yourself, they will take it from there, always trying new variations for themselves and progressing as they refine their techniques. All it will take from an adult is provision of the materials, and the first time help to get going. This activity will offer such peaceful work that parents will find themselves reluctant to leave it and will soon be hooked themselves.

• • • • •

spattering

Spattering appeals to the child in all of us! Old toothbrushes and a popsicle stick or other wooden spatula are needed for this. Spattering does what it says — it spatters a huge area, larger than a sheet of paper, so make sure that the table or floor is covered with newspapers before starting.

Dip the brush into the paint (powder paint,

spattering may be done inside a large carton — there will be less chance of overspray

poster paint) and shake off any excess. Then draw the wooden spatula gently over the bristles while holding the brush facing down over the paper. The bristles will flick and send droplets of paint flying on to the paper. After a little practice this can be controlled and a fine mist or heavy dots produced.

To screen off some parts of the paper, make stencils of cut shapes which will cover the paper and prevent spattering drops covering the area. Stick these stencils in place with an adhesive which allows you to lift it off later, or reposition it. When one colour is dry, screen off a design and spatter again with a second colour. Try spattering through a mesh screen.

folding combined with spattering

For an interesting effect, scrunch up a sheet of paper and then unfold it lightly. Do not flatten completely. The paper now has peaks and valleys with deep creases and smooth patches. Spatter on to the paper from one angle only. The paint will highlight the pattern of the folds. If you have an aerosol can of paint this is a good technique to try, but always work in a well-ventilated place. Open out flat and lay to dry . . .

indian ink bubbles

Dilute indian ink with a little washing up liquid and paint a design with this on a sheet of glass. The ink will break up into a bubbly dotty texture. Lay a sheet of paper on top and take a print. Lift off carefully and leave to dry.

• • • • •

spraying

For older artists spraying is an exciting challenge. There are two things to bear in mind, though: work must be done in a well-ventilated place, and every surrounding surface must be covered as the spray flies far and wide. Aerosol spray paints are not cheap, and so should not be squirted haphazardly simply for the hell of it. All paints soluble in water are suitable if applied thinly. There is a blower for spattering available in art shops which gives a spray result. Control spray by laying the work inside a large carton, from which you have cut away one side.

Spray directly on to paper or through a fine screen, such as nylon mesh from old stockings or tights, or even muslin. Parts of the design may be masked off by sticking cut-out shapes or stencils on to the work; use an adhesive which allows you to lift off and reposition shapes as you like.

Try repeating the same shape again and again, overlapping, at different angles, and in varying shades of colour. Then perhaps try a picture in which some areas are sprayed while some are masked: waves, skyscapes, sunsets or mountain peaks might suggest ideas. There is a big difference in effect between masking with pieces of paper roughly torn into shapes, and those cut accurately with scissors. Do a few experiments – misty clouds are better torn, a flying bird may be better cut out.

See Folding combined with Spattering above, and try this with spraying.

tie-dye or fold and dip

The art of tie-dyeing is centuries old and wonderful patterns are made when tight knots made in the fabric prevent the dye from reaching some areas of cloth. These knots can be made by tying areas of cloth around little stones with string. When the cloth is knotted all over, the cloth is dipped into the dye. This dye will only reach parts of the fabric not too tightly knotted or folded. In this way some areas are left undyed and they form the design.

A paper dipping method can be tried which uses the same principles. Using various papers found around the home – greaseproof paper, kitchen towel, tissue paper and paper napkins – experiment with folding the paper repeatedly into tiny knife pleats and clip them closed with a clothes peg. When this paper is dipped into fountain pen ink, some areas where the pleats are very tight will not take up the ink. When you open the paper out to dry, a design will have been made with some areas untouched by the ink and others with lighter or darker shades of ink, depending on where it has soaked in.

If you do not have a clothes peg you can use a bulldog clip. Alternative clips are girl's hair grips and paper clips.

Different effects result from opening the paper out to dry soon after dipping, or alternatively leaving it to dry with clips in place. The first method gives some running and smudging of the ink, but this can be attractive.

printing

You can take prints off a variety of everyday objects, or create new designs from cutting out shapes on halved potatoes or building up blocks of polystyrene. Other materials from which printing blocks can be made range from wood and cork to lino. Printing focuses attention on textures and surfaces and is a new and exciting avenue to explore for children who cannot draw particularly well. Through printing they can express an artistic idea, experiment and discover.

Apply paint to the block with a brush or a roller, or by pressing the shape on to a sponge which has soaked up paint to form a pad.

You will need a rubber roller (available in art and craft shops) and some printing ink. Home-made printing ink can be made cheaply by mixing one teaspoon powder paint with one teaspoon wallpaper paste (ready mixed). This should form a sticky gel-like paste. A sheet of glass should be used to spread the ink so that it coats the roller evenly. Put a blob of printing ink on the sheet of glass and then roll the roller over this. Now ink your block and take a print.

Prints taken from nature show in fine detail the structure of a leaf or feather. For these, simply ink the leaf or feather, using a brush, and then take a print by pressing the object gently on to the paper with a wad of newspaper. String and rope make exciting prints, alone or wound around a wooden block.

collage

a paler shade of grey

No one would think at first glance that a fascinating and subtle design could be made from boring looking newsprint, but this is how you do it. First, look carefully at a sheet of newspaper. There are areas that are completely black, some spots that are completely white, and in between these two are many shades of grey where the density of the printed letters makes it appear darker or lighter. By cutting out small square pieces from this sheet of newspaper, you will have 'mosaics' of different shades of white, grey or black. To make all your mosaic squares the same size you'll need to make a template or stencil from a piece of card. Cut this out within a larger piece of card so that it forms a 'window'.

Take a large bundle of newspapers and, placing your little window over the print, mark and cut out your squares in varying shades of grey, black and white. With a good supply of these mosaics young artists can make up a design by sticking them on to a large sheet of paper in graded shades and contrasts. Small shapes are the most effective: try little squares, hexagons or triangles.

multicoloured collages

Torn pieces from magazines, wrappers, silver foil, tissue paper and even cellophane can be used to build interesting collages. The pieces of paper can be torn or cut. The effect will be very different: either very precise and mosaic-like, or ragged and feathery on the edges with a soft blurred texture where you have torn the paper. Each method suits a different style of picture. For soft mountains seen through a mist, torn soft paper will give a foggy blurred outline. For a design of towering skyscrapers you might prefer to use cut out shapes for crisp lines on the building, and torn shapes for clouds in the background.

illusions
· · · · · · · · · · · · · · · ·

optical illusion

Baffle and delight some cooped-up kids with these revelations about illusion. They will probably go on to baffle you with their discoveries, drawings and experiments.

The first example is the fact that white circles seem bigger than black ones of the same size.

Take a sheet of black paper. Cut into a square, and then, within this square, cut out a circle. Place this black square with a circle in it on a sheet of white paper. Place the black cut-out circle on a sheet of white paper alongside. Now compare them. Even though you know that the black circle was cut from the black sheet, the white circle now seems bigger. To someone seeing them for the first time and not knowing how you cut them, this seems more marked.

Now try making other illusions with black and white paper using stripes.

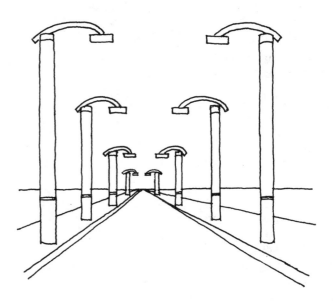

the illusion of distance

When we draw something in three dimensions we want to show the concept of distance. Some parts of the picture will be representing something further away from us than other parts.

Suggest your young artists take a good look at a road with a row of lamp posts. They seem to get smaller as they go further away. We draw objects that are identical in size in real life as though they are smaller in the distance on paper. If we did not, the picture would show that they were larger than all the others. Let them practise drawing a row of the same shapes going away into the distance.

illusion of depth

Perspective is the art of drawing on a flat sheet of paper in such a way that you make objects look solid.

Look at a cube: the secret technique is to remember that any lines that are parallel must be drawn to meet at a vanishing point somewhere in the background. You can place this point anywhere on the paper – with different effects.

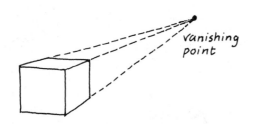

- A high vanishing point makes you feel as though you are looking down from above.

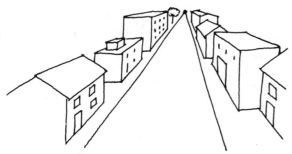

- To give the illusion that you're viewing the scene from nearer the ground, place the vanishing point lower, perhaps a little above halfway up the page.

- If you want to view the scene from ground level, place your vanishing point as low as you can.

- Placing the vanishing point on the edge of the page gives the illusion that you are looking at the scene from one side.

A vanishing point helps to make the picture appear to show depth, but also helps to indicate the eye-level at which you are looking at the scene. Try drawing the same object with the vanishing point placed in different positions.

Some pictures have two vanishing points, this does not make the perspective too difficult, simply remember that parallel lines must meet at a point.

• • • • •

illusion of length

Amazing but true! Two lines of exactly the same length can appear to be different lengths with the addition of other lines top and bottom. Take a look at these;

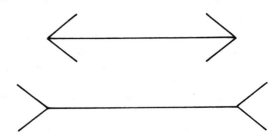

optical illusions in real life

As long ago as the 5th century BC, Greek building planners realised that certain optical illusions had to be corrected in their temple designs. They found that a sensitive eye could 'read' the lines as sagging and falling outwards! They made very sophisticated refinements in the design of the building as a whole, and of each element, to make it look as though it was absolutely straight and even. A photograph of the Parthenon in Athens will illustrate this for you.

To prevent horizontal lines above a row of columns seeming to sag, they made a slight rise or curve in these lines to correct this.

The upright columns lean slightly inwards at the top and each column has a convex or bulging shape, narrowing toward the top.

Without these changes, the columns would have appeared to fall outwards!

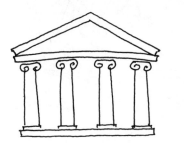

Picture mounts

In our own homes we can look at the example of a picture frame. Well-mounted pictures are placed on a mounting board which has a wider border on the lower edge than on the other three sides. This gives the impression that the picture is mounted in the middle of the mounting board. It is an optical illusion.

animation and cartoons

Animation is an attempt to capture and recreate movement through a series of drawings. Film cartoons and some adverts on television use this method. Sophisticated studios work on animated films, but anyone can produce a simple impression of movement by making a running cartoon.

running cartoon

In a running cartoon, movement is simulated by flicking the pages of a book. Try this with a little notepad or the corners of the pages of a soft exercise book. In a simple version a figure is drawn in the bottom right hand corner of each page, and is shown in two positions, on alternate pages. For example, if the figure is running, on the

first page the leading foot will be lifted and on the next this foot will be down. By repeating these drawings (tracing paper can be used for this), you will have the impression that the figure is running when you flick through the pages.

Some points that will help:

• Remember that a viewer will see the back pages first, so a figure coming towards you should seem to get larger. Start at the back of the book and draw the figure slightly larger on successive pages as you work forward.

• When drawing a sequence of movements, use a model of some sort – a Sindy, Barbie or Action Man doll could be posed. Animals, however, will never stay in one position! For them, speedy sketches or photographs might help.

- Offer young cartoonists some of these ideas to try out.
  A seagull flying and swooping.
  A cat licking itself.
  A mouse scampering.
  The stages of peeling a banana.
  A snake wriggling.
  A baby crawling.

You will see from this list that you can use more than two positions to show movement. If you choose to do a banana gradually being peeled, each drawing will show some progress until it is fully peeled in your last drawing.

strip cartoon

Could your cooped-up kids tell you an amusing tale in three or four boxes? It is quite a challenge. The idea of a good strip cartoon is to be clear and amusing in a few simple stages.

Draw the boxes or frames on white paper. Use a second transparent sheet to help re-draw the figures a second or third time, keeping certain characteristics the same each time, such as the hair and clothes, or the scenery. All the drawings are usually the same size unless the figure is disappearing into the distance.

Take one of these simple basic ideas and practise it in different ways.

- An aeroplane doing aerobatics and falling.

- A bee buzzing about and stinging.

- A boy giving his mother a nasty surprise.

In all of these there is a question to be asked. The answer will give the twist to the tale. Where does the aeroplane fall? What does the bee sting? And finally, what does the little boy give his mother?

Children enjoy thinking up twists to old stories. Fairy tales for example can have a modern element inserted and they will seem funny. Rapunzel could not let down her long hair if it was permed into a frizz or spiked with gel like a punk!

Many cartoonists look at well-worn stock phrases with a new eye and manage a joke from something familiar to us all.

Another way of creating a joke is to use animals in a human way. A suitable animal can be made to say a well-known human phrase. In the right setting it can seem hilarious.

art and design

camouflage

Small children are discovering the animal world with excitement. They are entertained by the remarkable camouflage some creatures assume. Talk about camouflage, why it is necessary, and what it means to blend in with the background.

Try this project for some lighthearted fun. Collect some discarded magazines. Look for coloured, patterned, stippled, furry, streaky, or spotty parts of pictures and tear them out. Paste one of these pieces on to a sheet of drawing paper and then design and paint a background for it so that it is well camouflaged. It should be difficult to see the original piece if you step back a little and view the work from a distance. Can friends find the first piece?

ancient art

In books or pictures you can give a child a closer look at Egyptian art or Greek vases, noticing the decorative designs on them. Trace the outline of a vase or column and suggest the child fill in his or her own version of the designs used to decorate it. A story might be depicted, a war, a hero's actions, or a scene from mythology.

Notice how strict the Egyptian style was; all artists had to follow the same 'rules' – seated statues have their hands on their knees; men have darker skin than women. Which way do the heads face?

In what ways did the Greek artists present people differently?

design for today

Have a good look at some dinner plates and then cups and saucers and a teapot. Could you design your own patterns for chinaware? Discuss with the children your particular design needs and ask them how they would tackle the design of a large 12"/30cm round dinner plate. They might try a few ideas for a tall elegant jug and a round fat teapot. Regular geometric patterns all round or swirling curvy shapes, flowers, stripes and spots? This design will have to look good first thing in the morning, with food on it, on a table set for dinner, against a cloth or on a bare table. Take all this into account as you discuss the type of set they are going to produce.

Provide plenty of paper and fine brushes with watercolour paints. A few drawing aids such as a curve, a compass or even a stencil may be of help.

design a logo

A logo is an emblem or image that is used to represent a company or association. Discuss logos together and think of examples. There are sports teams who have them, brand names and school badges are a form of this. The logo serves as a symbol to tell us something about that group. It should be stylised, exciting, and suitable for printing on everything used by the company or group. You will have to think about its use on letterheads, carrier bags, shop fronts, rugby jerseys and vans. Some logos are a design made up of the initials of a name. Others represent what the group does.

Could your young design team tackle a new logo for a new local TV station, an anti-smoking campaign, a garden centre, a range of teenage fashion clothes (labels, carrier bags, shopfront, invoices) and a salvage company called Dare Devil Deep Sea Divers who look for treasure on the sea bed?

Use only one, or at most two, colours to do this as it is cheaper to print in one colour. Designers must consider these designs in different sizes as they will be needed for varied positions. Hold the work up in front of a mirror to get a fresh look at it from time to time.

design a poster

Posters are often read at a distance, or in a passing car, so their message must be eye catching and clear. Impact is the single most vital ingredient. A poster designer must be certain to include all the information needed. Set a few challenging poster ideas to a group of artists and they will come up with a wide variety of solutions. Choose themes relevant to their ages; a pop concert poster must give dates, times and details of where it will be held, where to book, and prices. Theatrical posters are often used as the basis for a design on a programme cover too so consider this possibility.

makes
•••••••••••••

make a map

A map, like a floor plan, is a bird's eye view. Your kids could enjoy drawing a map of your street and its surroundings. We often assume that roads are at right angles to one another, but this is most often found to be untrue. In the same way, when placing a building on a plot of land, we need to measure the distance from the walls to the boundary in several different places. With a number of young surveyors we have discovered that there is a variation from corner to corner in a building we all thought was built parallel to the road! Make a key to explain symbols such as traffic lights or bridges, and, of course, the scale of the map. Measuring may need to be in the form of large strides.

•••••

make a floor plan of your room

This is a useful thing to do. In this way you can 're-arrange' a room in several different ways with-

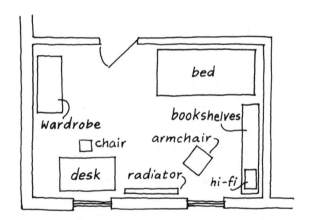

out the upheaval of the real thing. When you have worked out a good layout on paper, and corrected any mistakes, it will be simple to arrange the room like this.

There comes a moment when a child takes responsibility for the decorating and arrangement of his or her room despite never taking responsibility for the tidying of it! Drawing a floor plan allows you to consult each other over this new scheme, foresee and avoid problems, and sort things out well.

Give the child this working guide:

A plan is the view from above, looking down.

Show double lines for walls

(wider for outside walls)

Windows are shown

Furniture will be seen as if by a fly on the ceiling.

1 Measure the total length and width roughly first to make sure your plan will fit on to the sheet of paper when you have decided your scale.

2 Decide on your scale, e.g. 1in. = 1 yd.

3 Begin at one corner and slowly work around the room, marking doors and windows in their correct location. Measure and draw small sections at a time.

4 Make a note of the height of the windows from the floor, so that you know whether or not you can put furniture beneath them.

5 Note all electric plug points, radiators and water points (a basin?).

6 On another sheet of paper draw your furniture to scale.

7 Cut these out.

8 You might like to make a list of the good things about your room as it is now, and the things you think are wrong with it and need changing.

9 If you have a desk or table, is it in good light? Is your bed out of a draught? Are there long electric flexes trailing everywhere? If you have a great collection of records, work out how to store these.

By moving the paper furniture around your floor plan, you will gradually resolve these difficulties and find the best solution for your room. Even the greatest designers often make compromises! Not every room is ideal for its purpose. I think there is a challenge in making a good feature out of the worst problem in the room. My son chose to paint some exposed plumbing pipes in his room a bright shiny orange and this led to an exciting colour scheme.

make a simple rag book for a baby

Rag books are loved, gazed at and chewed. They are easy to make and will give some small person much pleasure, especially if made by an older brother or sister in a personal way.

Make certain that non-toxic fabric paints are used, and supply the child with a piece of cotton or linen fabric about 24″ × 8″/60cm × 20cm.

Briefly fold the book as it will be bound (see diagram), mark the edges of the pages, then open out flat and leave the artist to draw the pictures and paint them in.

Trim the edges with pinking shears, and bind the book with a few stitches.

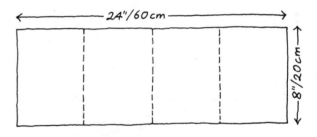

use non-toxic fabric paints

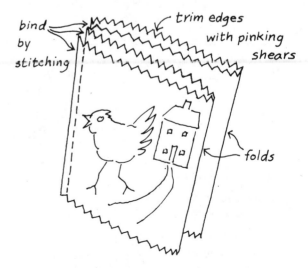

make a drawstring bag

Everyone can use one of these. Quick and easy to make, children can make them for their own use or as gifts. Scrap fabrics make colourful bags and other scraps may be used to appliqué names or words. Alternatively try fabric paints to paint on a name or design.

To begin, you will need to find a piece of fabric twice as wide as the bag you require, for the fabric will be folded in half. The length should suit the purpose of the bag.

Follow diagrams for a simple quick make.

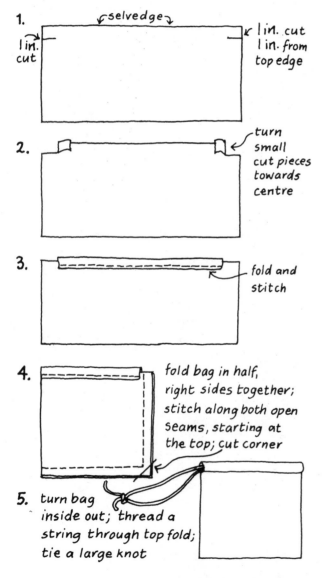

1. selvedge
1 in. cut
1 in. cut
1 in. from top edge

2. turn small cut pieces towards centre

3. fold and stitch

4. fold bag in half, right sides together; stitch along both open seams, starting at the top; cut corner

5. turn bag inside out; thread a string through top fold; tie a large knot

make log cabin patchwork

Quilts worked in the simple and easy American log cabin patterns are a reminder of a pioneer way of life in the Wild West. Isolated on the frontier, the settlers used what materials they had again and again if possible, cutting up scraps of fabric from used clothing to make into cosy bedspreads. The log cabin design is based on the way that the logs are laid in a log cabin, but they also echo earlier variations of this pattern seen on mummy wrappings in Egypt and in mosaic tiled floors.

The cabin in the woods symbolised shelter for the family in the wilderness, and the quilts, too, have symbolic meanings. The strips represented the logs which the pioneer used, and the centre square represented the heart of the home. Red squares symbolised the chimney, warmth and comfort, while yellow squares glowed like lanterns.

Quiltmaking has traditionally been done in groups and it was common for people to work on one quilt together. One adult working with a group of children can produce some very lovely and original work. I have made a quilt with a group of boys and girls of five and six years old.

It is helpful if needles are threaded up beforehand by the adult, and the cotton thread doubled and knotted so that the child is sewing with a double thread. Needles do not constantly become unthreaded and lost. Very fine sewing is not needed, simple running stitch is used. Aim to be fairly even in stitch size and draw seam lines with a ruler in pencil if it helps the child keep straight. This should be creative fun as the pieces are chosen and the colours blended. A child should not have to agonise over the stitching, but be encouraged to relax and make progress as part of the whole.

The design is the placing of constant width but gradually inc around the centre square in concen

Allocate one or two children as cut job is to cut long lengths of logs as wide as width from the fabrics you are using.

1 Begin with a square of 1"/2.5cm. Join the first log to the square along one edge, right sides together. Cut the log to the exact length of the square after it is sewn on.

2 Now open out the log and square and lay flat. Take a second log and join, face down, to the square and first log, with a seam at right angles to your first.

3 Cut log 2 to the length of the square plus log 1 and then open out.

4 Continue adding logs around the central square, always seaming at right angles to the previous seam, and trimming the length of the log after it is joined to the work.

It is traditional to put strips of a darker shade on two adjacent sides of your patchwork square, and lighter ones on the opposite two sides. When you come to join completed squares together, patterns are created by the juxtaposition of these dark and light areas as dark and light 'diamonds' form.

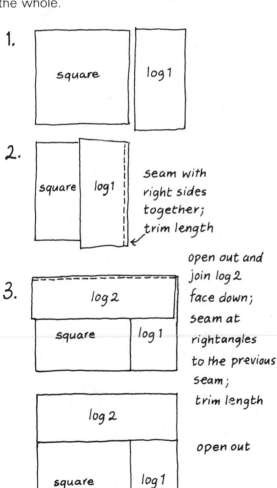

1.

square · log 1

2.

square · log 1

seam with right sides together; trim length

3.

log 2

square · log 1

open out and join log 2 face down; seam at rightangles to the previous seam; trim length

log 2

square · log 1

open out

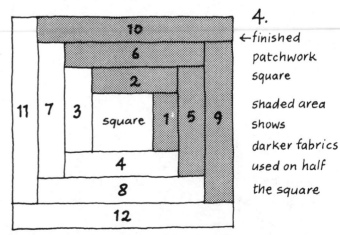

4.

← finished patchwork square

shaded area shows darker fabrics used on half the square

... strips (logs) of a
...reasing length
...ric rings.
...ers. Their
... a ruler

...g into shape, clay
... ne top of my list.
... material in your
...ple, and children
... it into sausages
...thumbnails into it!

. . . . .

playdough

Keep this dough in a plastic tub in the fridge.

1 mug of cold water
1 mug plain flour
½ mug salt
1 tablespoon vegetable oil
2 teaspoons cream of tartar
colouring (optional)

Mix all the ingredients together and form a smooth paste. Place in a saucepan and cook slowly until the dough forms a ball. Allow to cool and then knead for a few minutes. If you add colouring at the kneading stage you will produce streaked marbled dough.

...modelling
. . . .

papier mâché

Perhaps this is the messiest activity of all, but children love it and it can be used for a wide variety of modelling ideas. Use papier mâché to create model railway landscapes, slowly building up layers to form hills and valleys. Or apply the papier mâché layers to a blown up balloon and remove it when dry, leaving a mask curved to fit your head. (Be sure to remove all bits of balloon as they are dangerous if swallowed.)

Tear up several newspapers into tiny pieces and soak thoroughly in a bucket of hot water to soften. Then, with both hands, rub the bits into a pulp and squeeze out the moisture. Strain and wring in a cloth. Mix with the following paste recipe and model before the mixture becomes dry.

paste

½ mug flour
1 tablespoon salt
cold water

Put in a small pan and add water until it has the consistency of thick cream. Bring slowly to the boil and simmer, stirring for 5 minutes. Keep in an airtight jar in the fridge.

Mix this paste with the paper pulp to form lumps such as noses or raised areas in a landscape. For other flatter parts of the work, use layers of torn up paper and paint on the paste between each layer of paper. In this way you can build up layers gradually, using small pieces of paper to keep control of your work.

Where you build up layers on a mould or form, such as a glass bottle, cover your mould with a wet cloth first to prevent the papier mâché sticking too firmly to it. Then it will be easy to detach after the layers have dried.

fun and fantasy

'From the capacity to dream springs
the very progress of the human race.'
Jim Trelease Read Aloud Handbook
Penguin 1982

'Tell me a story', 'Make me into a clown', 'I want to be a magician!' These requests are heard by parents everywhere. Look here for ideas on telling and using stories, dressing up and acting, making disguises and trying out a few magic tricks.

A child can become a pirate with a twirling moustache and then switch to a wizard with a swirling cape. In the world of fantasy children can prick balloons and they won't pop, they can give commands to a floating cork and be obeyed! Nothing is impossible!

Within the pages of this section are secret methods for transforming children into monsters with claws on their feet, for changing their body shape from two legged to four, for instant manes and for growing a tail. To ease your task very ordinary objects around the home plus a child or two are transformed into these weird and fantastic creatures.

stories
· · · · · · · · · · · · ·

Stories serve to teach, inspire, warn, comfort and entertain every generation. A sense of heritage and culture is transmitted to our children through stories, along with glimpses of worlds other than our own. The imagination can take flight in a good story, and the concentration required can provide a complete relaxation from the problems of the day.

Children's listening skills develop as you read regularly to them. They unconsciously increase their vocabulary, develop comprehension skills and see themselves in situations from the story.

· · · · ·

reading aloud

The first and most obvious way to enjoy stories together is to read aloud to children. Sharing the magic of the words, the suspense and the excitement, plus, hopefully, beautiful high quality illustrations, will lead to a life-long love of books. As children show an interest in reading, some experts suggest that you point to the word as you go along so that a watching child can follow and gradually come to recognise which shapes produce distinctive sounds. Later, the child may delight in reading to you and to younger non-readers.

It can be helpful to early readers if you record a favourite story very slowly and clearly on tape, pausing between phrases, so that the child can listen over and over again following in the book or not as he or she wishes.

Some children come to believe in the existence of the characters and will enjoy acting out a story they have loved. Simple disguises such as hats and masks or a long skirt can be adapted from the dressing up box (see pages 87–88).

recording

To keep a story on tape for future listening sessions, a recording can be made. For this, the performers will need to think carefully about what sounds they can produce. Grand gestures with arms out-flung will be useless in this context, though galloping horses' hooves (fingers drumming on the table) or footsteps in the snow (crunching salt) can be sensational.

Have a practice run first to make them aware of how far to stand away from the microphone. Everyone should take care not to knock it inadvertently. Eager musicians can provide mood music in the background (the most popular seems to be the frightening sort indicating danger – thin, tremulous string!). Simple percussion is very effective for punctuating the story with jumps, big blows and crashes.

Bells or chimes might mark the midnight hour; train scenes can be easily achieved with various clicking sounds and a whistle.

Doing the story this way adds a new dimension as the wind whistles and the waves crash on the shore. Enterprising older children will be prepared to roam around with a tape recorder, picking up a library of sounds from real life to use later. To 'edit in' the sounds, a second recorder will be needed.

sound experiments

- Crumple cellophane.

- Rub a wet finger round the rim of a glass to obtain a whining sound.

- Fill bottles to different levels with water and tap with a spoon.

- Hit a glass lightly with a spoon.

- Record a clock ticking.

- Record birdsong outside.

- Record a car approaching, passing and disappearing.

- Record water pouring, dripping and gushing.

- Try speaking in different voices.

- Sound is magnified when sound waves travel along a wooden table. Put a watch at one end, or jangle keys and record the sound at the other end.

- If near the sea, try to capture the sound of the waves breaking and gulls screeching. Could this be simulated if you are not by the sea?

- Try to simulate thunder and rain. Rattle a baking sheet or a lego base board for thunder. Foil trays and sheet make useful sounds, and rice falling on to this sounds like rain.

- Listen to the sound of rice falling on different surfaces.

•••

waterscape

The sounds of the sea can be made by whooshing and whistling through the teeth and by using water itself. Prepare a large washing up bowl and provide jugs and mugs, old squirter bottles, milk bottle tops and a sponge. The milk bottle tops are laid on the bottom of the bowl, which is then filled with water. If a hand is drawn through these, or merely over them, they give a sound like the pebbles under the water being moved by the current. Pourings and spillings, gurgles and bubbles can be added together to create the sounds of the sea. Using a tape recorder, players can check how they sound, and make adjustments. This makes an excellent background noise for a recorded story about the sea. Simply lowering the squirter bottle into the water will cause it to fill and bubbles of air will escape. This happens too with the sponge. Experiments will perfect these techniques. Try to recreate the sound of water amongst the rocks, splashing. Try a regular wave, and don't forget the wind and gulls.

•••••

vocabulary

Look for unusual words in a story and discuss them together. Try to use them in another sentence, then think of other words that mean the same thing or something similar. Ask questions such as, 'Could you say the same thing in another way?', 'Do you think the author has expressed the idea very well?', 'Why?' Check on the child's comprehension by asking questions about the actions and thoughts expressed.

Some parents complain of TV-addicted kids never reading. For such a child, think of other ways to use language and build skills. Ask this child to write down the story of a favourite programme, carefully describing what happened. Perhaps an episode of the child's own life could be made into a story. Writing in the form of dialogue, rather like the style of the TV shows, suits some people better than a descriptive style.

TV script

Older writers could attempt a TV script dealing with an exciting event, sport, news, discovery, or if their interest is wildlife, the habits of an animal.

• • • • •

family magazine

Telling a story is a talent. A family magazine or news sheet can be made up of small 'articles' written by members of the family, the odd photo, drawings and headlines. This might take the place of 'duty' letters to far-off relations and would be fun to produce and to receive.

design and direct

Offer the child a basic 'script' and describe where the action takes place. The child then searches old magazines, photos, Christmas cards, etc for suitable pictures with which to illustrate the story. Pictures are cut out and pasted on card. Tiny pieces of Velcro or sandpaper are glued to the back of each picture. Cover a board with a piece of felt. With this set of moveable characters and scenery the child can arrange scenes and move the characters about at will. The Velcro will hold the pictures firmly in position on the background board.

dressing up ...

• •

Become another person, let go all inhibition! Dressing up is the first step towards changing into a different person or animal. It's fun from the moment you pull the first shiny piece of material out of the dressing up box, and a child begins to believe in the new reality. I can think of no other activity which gives almost more enjoyment in the preparation stages than in the end result. The times you fall about laughing at each other as children transform themselves (and parents too), with mixed-up combinations of clothes tried on before settling for *the* look – all this plus ingenuity, the challenge of substitution and the need to make something quickly and cheaply, makes keeping a dressing up box a must.

For special needs I have given a few outfits which can be made up quickly and cheaply for a party or a play. But in the dressing up box used for daily play the requirements are a little different. The items need to be simple enough to serve in many guises; they are mostly things you would otherwise be throwing away. Children should be able to put them on alone and safely.

the dressing up box

A few useful dressing up basics:

● Old shoes that are far too large for children, high platform heels and men's shoes suitable for clowns and tramps.

- Face paints, non toxic.

- A piece of the cheapest, nastiest, shiniest red satin bought as a remnant is worth its weight in gold. This becomes a royal prince's cape, a martian's tunic, or even a red rag to a bull when held in the hands of a bull fighter.

- Discarded nylon tights. These can be variously worn on two legs or four: for donkeys, and doublet and hose. Once some children made a great monster, rather like an octopus, which came down a flight of stairs with four legs and four arms encased in a variety of tights. I have also seen an effective mosquito with many hairy legs made from stuffed tights. Tights are ideal also for tails. Stuff one leg of a pair, cut off the other leg and keep the waistband. Tie a wool tassle on the end and wear your tail in comfort. Stuff discarded tights and use them to alter a child's body shape. They can become bosoms and bottoms as required! Stuff a leg and tie in the centre with string to form two bulges. Use the other leg to go around the child's chest to secure these matronly breasts in place.

- Strong large brown paper bags. These are safer than plastic, which must never be put over the head. They are easy to cut, paint and glue or staple together for use as masks.

- Hats of every sort, along with caps and wigs. Unused coarse wool can be made into any sort of hair from manes to wigs.

- Masks, keep any you might have made in the past.

- A shawl, a marvellous multi purpose item.

- An old sheet for ghosts, Roman togas, cloaks, camps, tents, saris . . . you name it.

- A piece of net for a bridal veil and for a princess or queen. A few spangles or sequins glued or sewn on to a piece of net makes it extra special.

  An old adult skirt and old adult pair of trousers. Belts and suspenders to keep these up.

- A square cotton scarf, for a pirate or a peasant girl.

- The odd cardboard sword and dagger.

brown bag horse

- Old socks. When not worn as socks, they can be painted, have paper scales or feathers attached to them, and, best of all, they can be given 'claw' attachments. Cut claws from plastic bottles where the curve of the base meets the upright side, cutting the flat bit of plastic extra wide to act as an inner tab securing each claw in a little hole in the sock. Stuff the sock so that real toes do not become scratched by the plastic tabs. Socks can be worn as caps on heads and on hands.

plastic
bottle –
cut out
claw

- Cotton wool can serve as a beard or as royal ermine.

use this pattern to cut
pirate's moustache
from black card

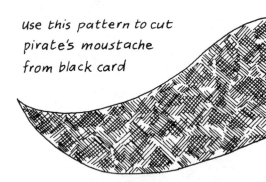

- Black card can be cut into witch's hats, moustaches, and black eye patches as well as simple masks.

- A long length of material will do service as a robe, tunic, cloak or general draped covering. Use an old tablecloth or discarded piece of curtain.

- Heaps of old newspapers are useful if you have storage space. The pages can be shaped into amazing fantasy headgear, hats or long spirals of 'hair'. Paper can also be torn up for papier mâché masks, or complete heads can be easily made by shaping papier mâché over a balloon.

Witches, tramps and clowns are quick, cheap and easy themes. They are reasonably scruffy and can be made from oddments and scraps. The child doesn't need to stay clean, so there are no worries about messing up a prized outfit. All are sexless, as witches can become wizards at the wave of a wand, and, best of all for the kids, they require a dirty or made-up face!

A simple hat making method will be useful in many dressing up themes. Light card and art papers are glued or stapled quickly to form headgear.

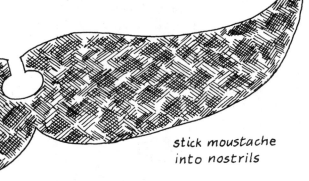

stick moustache
into nostrils

tramps

These characters are generally thrown together from old clothes that by rights should belong or have belonged to someone a few sizes larger than the child you are transforming. Dad's oldest pyjamas or shirt, cut down old jeans, a few patches sewn on haphazardly, a scruffy felt hat and a carefully mucky face. Stuff over-large shoes with newspaper or old socks so that they don't fall off. Hoist up huge trouser waists with belts or braces. Mess up hair, dirty hands.

30-minute witch

You need:
Black leotard, black tights
Black card, luminous yellow/green card
black tissue paper
Stapler, pair of scissors

The child wears a black leotard and black tights. Make a large hat with a conical top (see hat-making instructions). This should be made from black card, and the underside of the brim is spectacular made from luminous yellow-green card which throws an eerie greenish tinge on to the skin of the wearer. For a skirt, staple strips of black tissue paper on to a waistband made from a thin strip of the luminous card.

Hideous make-up, and hair braided into as many thin braids as possible, complete your witch. Any rubber spiders or mock cobwebs you may have in the house make useful extras, and a black wand can be added.

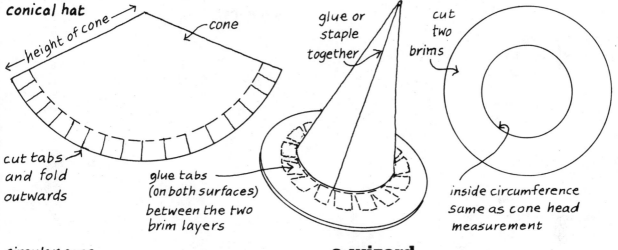

conical hat

height of cone

cone

cut tabs and fold outwards

glue tabs (on both surfaces) between the two brim layers

glue or staple together

cut two brims

inside circumference same as cone head measurement

circular cape

1.

Fold a large square of fabric in half and then in half again

2. Draw a curve (A) from corner to corner; draw a curve (B) to form the neck opening

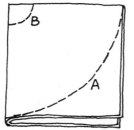

B

A

a wizard

Use the same hat and tights as the witch, plus a lightweight black poloneck jumper. Add a cloak, made from a piece of satin (black with red lining), the cheap shiny sort you may have in your dressing up box. See the instructions in the diagram.

neck

braid

ribbon

cut open

3. Cut along the two curved lines: you now have a circular shape with a hole in the centre

4. Cut open to the neck; hem neck edge and thread ribbon through hem fold; trim edges with braid

30-minute clown suit

This is a quickly made, effective fancy dress outfit made from a sheet of cartridge paper, tissues and crepe paper. It works out very cheap to make.

The impact will depend on the colours you choose, and the general shape of the clothes used. The child will wear some basic clothing so choose this first. Pay attention to a colour scheme and to the baggy trousered shape (run elastic around the ankles of large loose trousers). Striped socks, a waistcoat and a large shirt will complete the clothing, alternatively use a jumpsuit.

You will also need:
a sheet of heavy drawing paper, or card in a colour
    to match the clothes
stapler
elastic
a box of tissues, two-tone coloured
adhesive tape
2 packs crepe paper, different colours, for ruffle
needle and thread
glue

to make the hat
Take hold of one corner of the heavy drawing paper and roll it into a cone that will fit the child's head. Check for size before stapling. Measure a length of elastic for the chin strap and staple in place.

pompoms
These are fluffy bundles of the tissues gathered up to form a rosette shape. Lay tissues one on top of another, and gather up the centre. Twist adhesive tape firmly round and staple one at the top of the cone, then glue three more down the front of the hat. Attach pompoms to socks or shoes, down the front of the jumpsuit or waistcoat and at the knees with needle and thread.

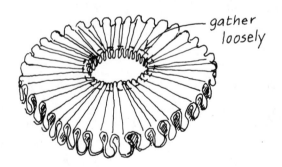

gather loosely

ruffle
Cut a strip 6"/15cm wide from each colour pack of crepe paper. Gather loosely with a huge tacking stitch using double thread. Place the ruffle around the child's neck and join with a stitch or two. Note: crepe paper has a tendency to lose its colour over everything if wet; beware drinks being spilt all over it.

Make up the face with face paints.

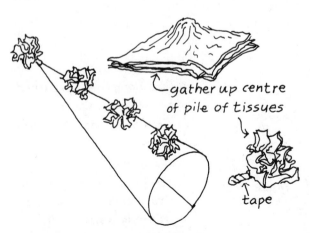

gather up centre of pile of tissues

tape

magic

How often do we wish for magic powers, merely the granting of one little wish! I must disappoint you here: I have no magic formula to offer except the power of imagination. But there are certain magic tricks we can all learn. Practice is always important, but simple tricks will give fun and entertainment. An adult can turn a few tricks and entrance a group of children, and children can do them to entertain each other.

magic power

1 Rub an inflated balloon vigorously against human hair, your own or a child's convenient head. Then hold the balloon against the wall of a room. It will cling to the wall. This works on walls painted with emulsion paint.

2 The electricity in our hair can also be used to charge a comb which can then be drawn over other people's heads a little distance above the hair. In response, their hair will stand on end and wave, following the magnetic pull of the comb.

3 You could use the previous trick to do a snake charmer's act with a piece of cotton thread. Charge the comb by vigorously rubbing it through your hair, then draw it in an arc over a piece of thread held upright in your hand. The cotton thread will sway from side to side and bend to your command. (Recharge the comb often.) At the start, the tip of the thread should face upward.

magic strength

This is for a child to do on a second unsuspecting child. The first holds a broomstick horizontally with two hands, palms down, hands 12"/30cm apart. The other stands opposite and takes hold of the broomstick by placing a hand on either side of the first child's hands, and tries to push the first child backwards. While this is happening, to counter the push, the first child should pull hard upwards. This gives him or her the strength required to resist being pushed over backwards.

magic matchbox

This is an old trick, but there are always new young victims who don't know it. Straighten your fingers and pinch up the loose skin on the back of your hand. Catch a piece of this skin immediately behind the knuckles and squeeze it into the matchbox, closing the box so that a piece of skin is closed inside it. Now, when you bend your fingers towards your palm, this skin will stretch, pulling the matchbox upright. Straighten your hand and it will lie down again. After you have done this for a child who loves it, show how it is done so that he or she may entertain many friends with the trick.

magic face

With a small handbag mirror you can distort some pictures. Place the mirror vertically in the middle of a picture of a face which is lying flat on the table. See this 'bend' the face and the expression. Slide the mirror slightly for another version.

magic patterns

Also a trick with a little mirror. Draw a repeat pattern on a piece of paper and fold it in half rather like a greetings card. Stand the card on the table, with the pattern on the inner sides. Put the mirror down so that it fits neatly into the right angle made by the two sides of the card. Now the pattern will seem to go on repeating into the distance.

Stand two mirrors against each other at right angles and place a pattern on the table between them. Another endless pattern can be seen.

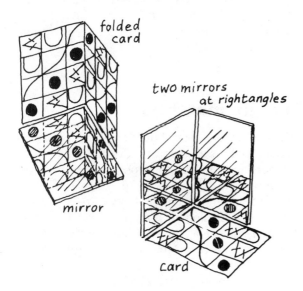

folded card

two mirrors at rightangles

mirror

card

magic numbers

Over the centuries many people have believed that the number 7 has magical powers. For the child who knows this trick, it may be true. On dice, the numbers on directly opposite sides to each other always add up to 7. Once he or she knows this, a performer will always be able to tell which numbers are face down on any throw of the dice. A little maths practice, then try this trick with first two dice and then three or four. An audience will be amazed that this young magician can tell how many dots are face down.

balloon popping

Place a strip of clear tape on a blown up balloon before the 'audience' arrives. Show them this inflated balloon. Suggest to them that this balloon has magic qualities because you will prick it with a pin and it will not pop or deflate. Do this by pricking the balloon on the tape. It will not pop, but air will very gradually leave through the tiny hole. Others from the audience may try this, but anyone pricking the balloon will pop it if you hold the taped side towards you.

NB Keep a firm grip on the pin and only use one with a big head. Don't be tempted to use a toothpick with two sharp ends: the force of the balloon popping can actually push this back into your finger.

• • • • •

magic cork

Fill a glass with water to the very top so that the water appears to be standing above the rim, bulging upwards. Put a cork very gently on the surface and watch how it goes to the centre even if you command it to stay at the edge. But if there is a little *less* water in the glass and the cork is commanded to stay in the centre, it will go to the edge!

NB After first showing how it will not go to the edge, pick up the cork (with a little water) and shake it before putting it back into a lower level glass of water.

flying paper

Fold a piece of paper into a tight wad and put this into the mouth of a bottle. Challenge a child to blow it further in – it will fly out instead.

• • • • •

a challenge

It is impossible to fold a piece of paper in half more than eight times. This is true whatever size and thickness paper you use. Try it out with a group: folds must halve the paper wad, but can be in any direction.

disappearing ring

Cut a long strip of paper about 1"/2.5cm wide and about 2'/60cm long. Give it a half twist and glue the ends together rather like a figure 8. This is called the magic Mobius strip.

Pierce the paper gently, and cut along the middle of the strip in order to cut the ring in half. Follow the curve of the paper. When you return to the beginning, instead of having two rings, each half as wide as the first, which is what you might have expected to find, the second strip will have disappeared completely and you will be left with one much longer ring.

This will fascinate watchers, and they too will soon be making and cutting strips for their friends to puzzle out.

This can be tested another way. Start painting one side of the paper red. Go around to where you started. Can you colour the other side another colour?

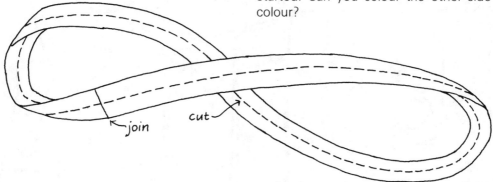

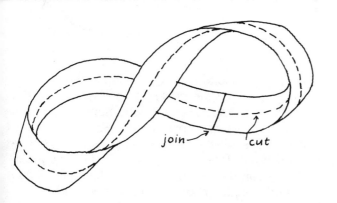

Next, try this version of the Mobius strip. Make a double twist in a length of paper and join with glue. When this strip is cut in half along its length, it will fall into two interlocking rings.

sound
and
rhythm

Sound and rhythm exist in nature even where there are no men around to hear them. Waves roll endlessly to shore; babies in the womb are exposed to the beat of their mother's heart. From the earliest times man has added his efforts at rhythm and sound to those of nature.

What is sound? In talking with children about sound their eager questions make us marvel again at the miracle of sound. A sound in the midst of silence is like the ripples on still water when a pebble is dropped into it. The ripples or waves travel outwards from the centre. Sound waves are vibrations which are set up and travel (like those ripples) at differing speeds. The human ear can hear sounds on a range of about 15,000 to 20,000 vibrations per second. Some will be loud, others extremely soft. The number of vibrations per second is termed frequency. The greater the frequency, the higher the sound.

Twang a rubber band to show a child the vibrations and hear a sound. As the frequency slows, the pitch of the note is lower. Along with notes of different pitch, music involves patterns of rhythm. It is the combination of pitch and rhythm that gives a tune its distinctive sound.

You can create pitch and rhythm while singing and clapping in time with your hands or with an instrument.

In this section there are musical instruments to make and games to play with sound and rhythm. People of all ages from two to eighty-two derive pleasure from music and, whether they are part of the pop generation or not, they will find a natural affinity with games exploring sound and rhythm. Try to include music making and singing on your travels and while waiting around — any boring odd moments are made livelier by singing.

making musical instruments

Some of these instruments are made with simple objects you may have at home, in the kitchen or garden. Before kids start putting a band together, check on neighbours' tolerance!

comb and tissue paper mouth organ

Wrap a sheet of hard tissue paper (the shiny sort, used for wrapping) around a comb. Make sure it is tightly wound around the comb's teeth. Put it to your mouth and hum the tune you want to play. It will sound quite different as the vibrations build up.

tubes and pipes

If you hold a cylinder or a milk bottle or tumbler just below your lips and blow towards the back rim you will hear a note. Try this with any tubes to hand — even hosepipes will produce a note.

drinking straw whistles

It often needs a few tries to get this right, so you may have to scrap one or two early efforts. Suddenly you will get the knack of it and it will seem easy.

Take a paper drinking straw and a pair of scissors. Flatten 1"/2.5cm at one end of the straw between fingers and thumb. Cut the corners from this flattened end and re-open very slightly. Place this end well into your mouth and, as though you were saying the letter 'P', blow into your straw with dry lips. A low note is produced from a long straw, and this can be raised by snipping little bits off the end. With practice a scale can be played. Tune against a piano. When a straw suddenly stops producing a note — which happens mysteriously (I suspect they get moist) — take another and start again.

flatten one end

cut corners

musical straws, variations

When you have mastered the making of one musical straw, try this experiment and hear some of the many notes the breath can make.

1 First, blow with your straw into an empty tin. Now your breath is vibrating in the empty tin as well as in the straw. This raises the note slightly in a process called resonance.

2 You can also make several musical straws of graded lengths and join them together with tape to form an instrument. Flatten and cut one end to a point as before. Use five straws in all, cutting the second ¾"/2cm shorter than the first and each subsequent straw 3/4"/2cm shorter than its neighbour.

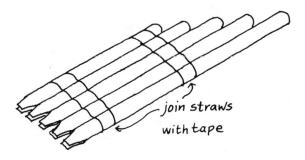

— join straws
with tape

3 Before joining them together, try blowing with each one into your empty tin. The shortest will produce the highest note.

4 Join them together by strapping them into line with sellotape. Blow into all five at once to hear a chord. Try this in your tin too.

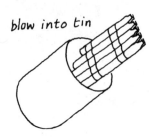

blow into tin

kazoo

A Kazoo is a very simple instrument – basically a tube with a hole in it and a tissue membrane stuck over the hole. It works best if you can compress or taper one end of the tube. From a cardboard tube, cut out a circle ⅞"/22mm in diameter and stick hard tissue paper (used for packaging) over the hole. Put the wide end to your mouth and hum or sing a tune through it.

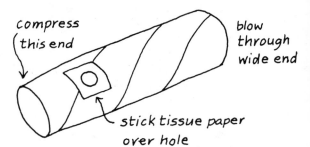

compress
this end

blow
through
wide end

stick tissue paper
over hole

whirling hose

A 3'/1m length of hosepipe whirled like a helicopter blade around your head will give an interesting sound. This will vary according to the speed with which you are able to move it.

• • • • •

is your body a wind instrument?

Children experiment with sounds like these the whole time, so try channelling them into a game.

How many raspberries and other cheeky noises can you make by blowing, using your teeth and tongue in various ways? Try clicks, pops, gurgles and whooshes. Whistle through your teeth, suck in and blow out. Snore and whisper. Pretend to be a gigantic machine and record your sounds on tape. Try to make a regular pattern of sounds, as would a machine.

elastic sound

Stretch rubber bands of different thicknesses over an empty shoebox without a lid. Pluck them to hear your own guitar.

Rubber bands may also be used stretched around the length of a ruler. Place a pencil across the ruler beneath the bands to form a 'bridge' and you now have a stringed instrument. Moving the bridge to another position on the ruler varies the sound. With a second pencil, make another bridge and try moving these two closer together and then farther apart; the sounds you will hear when you pluck the elastic bands are affected by this movement.

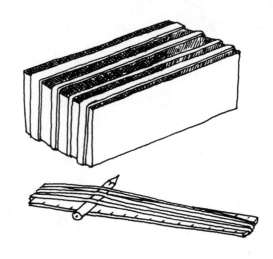

• • • •

human piano

With a group of musical people and a well-known tune you can produce a good sound.

Several people sit in a semi circle, facing one who shall be the player of the 'piano'. Each person represents one note and the player in the centre will *play* them by pointing to whoever represents the note he wants sung. Allocate notes to each person. It works well at first with a small group of five, but can obviously expand to an octave if you become expert at it.

When each person has been given a note, sing the scale through as Do Re Mi Fa So . . . to be sure of pitch. Now the central player chooses a tune, and will *play* it by pointing in turn to the notes needed. The 'notes' must sound instantly when pointed at. The easiest nursery rhyme tunes are good at first. The player can show with hand signals the length of note wanted and generally conduct to a tempo.

musical flowerpots

Clay flowerpots come in a range of sizes. They can be hung up in ascending size and used as chimes. To make different notes tap them with a wooden dowel.

Thread string through the draining hole at the bottom of the pot. Tie a large knot on the inside of each pot and hang them upside down by the string.

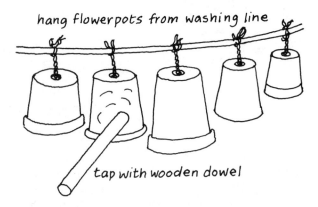

hang flowerpots from washing line

tap with wooden dowel

crashline

Suspend pots and pans from a washline with pieces of string. They should each hang and turn freely. Hit them or tap them with wooden and metal spoons.

● ● ● ● ●

milk bottle chimes

It is possible to produce the first notes of the D major scale using five 1-pint milk bottles. If you have another sort of bottle you will need to adjust the water levels carefully, tuning with a piano. If you are not worried about accurate notes, simply fill the bottles with gradually increasing amounts of water and tap with dowel rods for a delightful chime.

If you are after accurate notes, however, and have suitable bottles, you will need to make a little gauge with which to measure the water levels. Do this on a strip of cardboard. Measure and mark the water levels. Each level represents a note. Fill each bottle with the correct amount of water for that note. Line up the bottles in a row and you have a set of chimes.

It helps to stick coloured tape on to the bottles to mark the position of a note once you have found it. This way you can refill the bottles any time you wish without having to go through all the measuring again.

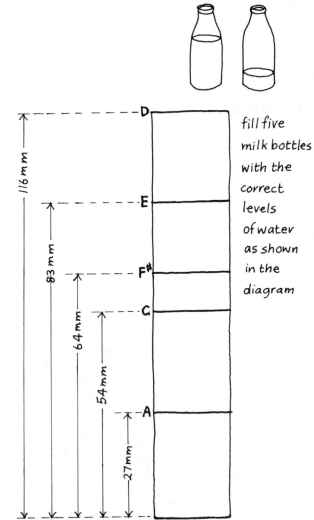

fill five milk bottles with the correct levels of water as shown in the diagram

more musical milk bottles

Strike a milk bottle with different spoons and listen to the different sounds they make. A metal spoon, a wooden spoon and a plastic spoon are easily found in the kitchen. Finally, bind a spoon by wrapping a little wadding around it and covering this with a piece of cloth, secured with an elastic band. Another way of muffling the striking surface is to wrap a Band-Aid, or any other adhesive strip, around the handle of the spoon, or, in the case of a teaspoon, to wrap an elastic band around it.

• • • • •

nail chimes

A series of nails hung by a thread from a frame will produce a delicate chime. Adult help is required.

Note: nails are bought in inch measurements, but, for accuracy, the sizes they must be cut to are given in millimetres. This may be confusing, but it seems unavoidable!

You will need, in all, five 6″ nails and four 4″ nails. The frame might be a wooden coat hanger or a simple wooden stand. Use the lightest thread possible (sewing thread is best).

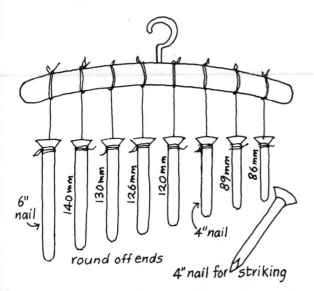

6″ nail

140mm 130mm 126mm 120mm 89mm 86mm

4″ nail

round off ends

4″ nail for striking

The nails are sawn at different lengths so that, when struck, they will sound at different pitches. An ordinary 6″ round nail will produce the note D, while a 4″ round nail will give the note B when struck. This is a good start. Saw off pointed ends of six more nails and file all rough edges giving a series of nails with the following lengths: 140mm, 130mm, 126mm, 120mm, 89mm and 86mm. The last two are cut from two 4″ nails.

Hang up the nails in size order when they are filed, and tap the chime with an extra nail. You will have a scale from the first keynote D which was made by the untouched 6″ nail.

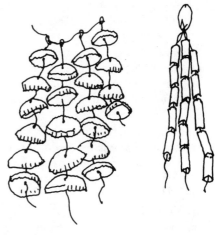

wind chimes

Collect old foil milk bottle tops and thread them on cotton sewing thread to make wind chimes which will rustle and tinkle. Macaroni pieces threaded up will also make a sound in the wind, rather a quiet clicking rustle.

• • • • •

cymbals

Pot lids are ideal, provided their owner agrees! Use only metal lids and aim for two of a similar size.

musical brushes

A wide range of sounds can be made with a selection of household brushes: tooth, bottle and wire floor brushes. Draw them over objects, pot lids suspended on a string, and over a baking sheet. Draw wire brushes around a plastic bowl. These will give excellent rhythmic background beats to songs and other musical efforts.

• • • • •

shakers

Fill jam jars ¾ full with thumb tacks, beans, nails or rice and screw on the lids tightly. These will make effective shakers to mark the beat. Empty cold drink cans may be filled too, and paper stuck firmly over the opening.

Explore not only the shake, rattle and roll rhythmic sounds of different contents, but experiment to see what can make their particular sounds change. For example, try shaking rice inside containers made from different materials. In a plastic one the sound will be distinctly different from the same quantity of rice in a metal tin. Then again, those same containers can be tried with beans or pebbles. Listen to the sounds made by seeds, macaroni, cereals and twigs. Seasonal shakers can be made with acorns and conkers, seedpods and dry leaves. All your variations can be tested with containers made of glass, metal and plastic.

You can change the type of sound produced from the shaker in several ways. I have talked about changing the container and changing its contents, but the sound is also varied by beating or hitting the shaker. Treat it like a drum and beat with a teaspoon, a wooden spoon and a plastic spoon. Muffle the striking instrument by twisting a rubber band around a spoon, or sticking a piece of elastoplast around it.

make your own drum

A piece of burst balloon stretched over a bowl or a pan will make a good drum. Alter the tension of the balloon by stretching it tighter or looser around the basin. Secure with an elastic band. Does this variation of tension alter the pitch? Could you tune these drums? Beat them with wooden spoons, metal spoons, plastic ones and spoons which have been bound with adhesive strips or covered with wadding and a piece of fabric to make a muffled sound.

There is a difference in sound between a closed drum and a drum open at the lower end.

bongo bin

Kids will enjoy playing bongo drums on various types of bin, upturned and held between the knees. On each, tap out a rhythm with the fingers, which should be held tightly together, hitting the drum with a flat slap. Exotic beats can be easily played using both hands at speed.

•••••

woodblock

Woodblocks can be made from a hollowed out coconut shell. An adult should accurately cut the coconut in half first and then the shells can be hollowed out. Hit them together.

•••••

spoons

Playing the spoons is a skilled business but well worth the practice you will need if you are to do it well. Hold two kitchen spoons back to back with a finger between the handles, and tap them against your other arm or knee to produce a castanet sort of rhythm.

•••••

rattlestick

With a little initial help from an adult to make the rattlestick, children can enjoy using it in musical games and general play. Take an old broomstick and lots of bottletops. Place two bottletops back to back and drive a nail through them, fastening them to the broomstick. Repeat this around the broom handle. It is a good idea to use long nails, not too deeply hammered in, so that the bottletops have room to move and clatter.

To play the rattlestick, hold it upright and thump on the ground, making all the bottletops rattle rather like a tambourine.

castanets

Nothing could be simpler than a piece of card folded in half with a metal bottle top stuck on to each half so that they click against each other when they are pressed closed.

Use stiff card, about 2½" × 5"/6cm × 13cm, make two folds in the centre of the strip of card, about 1cm apart. Glue the bottle tops on to each half, making certain that the edges of the bottle tops will collide.

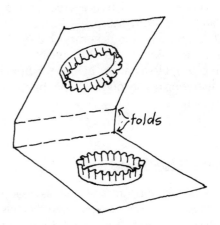

folds

bells on her toes

'She shall have music wherever she goes', if she ties little bells on her ankles or, like many tribal dancers, seed pods that rattle with each stamp of the foot.

•••••

washboard and thimbles

Washboards, once used for laundry, and an essential part of the skiffle music of the late 1950s and early 60s, are not always easy to find these days. But if an old one is still around, put a thimble on each finger of one hand and strum against the corrugated ridges. Try a wire brush drawn over the ridges for a regular beat.

exploring rhythm

Rhythm can be used in everyday life to make many types of work easier, and in sport to help a team work together. Talk with children about this and ask if they can think of other examples of situations where keeping in time is an important part of the activity. Together you may come up with dancing, rowing as a team, Tug of War type rope pulling, gangs of labourers working together, marching, and many more.

Children can try out some of these actions and put their own choice of rhythm to them. Is it easier to count to a pattern? Does the beat help to keep everyone going longer? What happens if the tempo increases?

follow the leader

If there is a group choose one as leader. The leader moves in a rhythmic pattern using his or her body to express this rhythm. All the others must keep in time with the leader and follow exactly. This can be done to music or simply by the leader counting. Try variations on step hops, and heel/toe taps, adding hand movements too.

music with muscle

Play a piece of music with a defined rhythm and let the players listen to it once carefully. The second time they 'join in' with the music, expressing through swaying or stepping their response to the music.

Once players have worked out movements to a phrase, try doing this as a round. With the first phrase, a couple of players make their movements, and when they go on to do the second phrase, the next two players join in doing their first phrase.

dance sequences

Make up a dance sequence to the rhythm, a repetitive pattern in which steps and arm movements are used to reflect a pulse-like beat. Pop and reggae are good for this, especially African and Caribbean music.

get carried away by rhythm

Imaginative swaying rhythms can transport us in our imagination as we become mesmerised by the movement. Kids can imagine themselves being trees swaying in the wind; now it is a hurricane . . .

Or they might be fronds of seaweed moved by the sea, washing on a line flapping in the breeze, leaves rustling on the trees, or the eternal flow of the sea tides.

rhythmic steps

The human body can move in various rhythmic steps. We walk, hop, skip and leap. Tap with fingers on a table the beat of someone walking, hopping and then skipping. Perhaps after hearing this, the children with you can do others – dance rhythms perhaps, the waltz or the polka? Do friends or family have particular walking rhythms? Sometimes you can tell who is walking down the corridor outside your room by the sound of their footsteps. Try this out and see if it is the sound of their shoes – high heeled taps or rubber soled squelches – that gives the clue, or the rhythm of the walking itself.

Recreate other rhythmic patterns with fingers on a table top so that others can guess what you have in mind. Do this with the sound of trains, galloping horses and machines.

walking, tramping, wandering,
loping, mincing, marching,
rambling, trudging, ambling,
pacing, meandering,
stamping, strolling

pendulum

There is a natural rhythm in a pendulum. Hypnotically, it swings back and forth. This rhythm varies according to the length of the string. Make a pendulum from a length of string with a stone or weight tied to it. Experiment with shorter and longer strings to give varied swings.

Swaying to the beat of the pendulum encourages an awareness of rhythm, rather like the beat of a metronome. There are many movements that can be done to this rhythmic pulse. Players might like to imagine that they are working on the railroad or chopping wood, and develop an action that fits in with the swing.

rhythmic patterns with words

Some words will fit rhythmic patterns. Choose a pattern quick-quick-quick-quick-slow-quick. Everyone tries to find words or names that fit this pattern. 'Piccadilly Circus' is one example. How many others can they find?

Long-short-short-short-long-short gave us 'scrambled eggs and bacon'. And an all-time favourite with kids is 'Yuckky stuff' from long-short-long with a quick rat-a-tat beat.

This is a marvellous game when stuck on a railway platform or waiting in an endless line, for feet can be shuffled to the beat, fingers can help tap out the rhythms, or hands can clap. This is a step towards enjoying poetry and appreciating the rhythm of words.

• • • • •

rhymes to fit rhythm

When sitting in the train, many of us hear words in the clickety clack, or imagine that in the roar of the waves at the shore we hear 'galoshes galoshes . . .' The famous little engine in the children's story said 'I know I can, I know I can' as he chugged up the hill pulling the heavy load. Words can be fitted to the sound of the Doctor's waiting room clock – or a background noise such as an air conditioning unit. Listen carefully to the many mechanical rhythms about the house; washing machines, too, have a 'voice'.

rhythmic names

This can be played as a game using the names of three people. The leader calls out three names, and the players must find another three names that fit the pattern of the syllables of the first three. 'Arthur, George and Mary' would be a pattern of long-short-long-short-long-short and this is echoed in 'Edward, Jane and Rory'.

Play this game with place names and sayings.

messages without words

A game to make someone understand you without words. The first player asks a question. This could be 'What did you have for lunch?', and the second claps the rhythm of the words he or she would have used. 'Sausages and bacon' would be /---/-.

The questions could be about song titles or TV show titles.

Trinidad and the big Mississipi, and the town Honolulu,
    and the lake
Ti ti ka ka, the Popacatapetel is not in Canada, rather in
Mexico, Mexico, Mexico...
Canada, Malaga, Rimini, Brindisi,
Canada, Malaga, Rimini, Brindisi,
Yes, Tibet, Tibet, Tibet,
Oh yes, Tibet, Tibet, Tibet.
Nagasaki and Yokohama
Nagasaki and Yokohama
Yes, Tibet, Tibet, Tibet. Oh yes,
Tibet, Tibet, Tibet.

be a lyricist

Some people simply have the knack of fitting words to music. Try short little phrases with a clear rhythm and ask children to fit words to these. Then gradually try doing this with longer tunes, and finally with complete songs. The music may be sung, or played on an instrument or tape recorder. Children of five have enjoyed fitting words to clapped rhythms of the a-rat-a-tat-tat variety. 'Three men in a hat' was the quick reply. Talk about where the stress falls in a word, what syllables are, and help the children to be aware of this. By the age of ten they might be composing the tune and writing the song!

There is more to being a lyricist than merely fitting words to rhythms as in an earlier game; here, the mood of the song is important, and the words should be easily sung and in their natural pronunciation.

games
for
groups

games

In different cultures throughout history games have evolved along similar basic lines. Strategic games requiring skill, logic and anticipation were exercises in survival. They were a mini form of man's struggle against nature and against other men. Testing and honing the powers of planning, foresight, resourcefulness and cunning, these games are contests which mirror real situations.

For children, games develop these skills while teaching them to play by the rules, to abide by a pre-agreed pattern for playing the game. Games may be substitutes for real battles and the hunt; they offer a harmless outlet for those aggressive feelings. Hidden in some games are struggles for supremacy, and children take them no less seriously than businessmen regard their strategic golf games.

The regard of your peers is a vital ingredient in your self esteem and children, no less than adults, need to prove themselves. Yet winning should not be allowed to become an obsession. Learning to play the game and 'be a sport' are still essentials, and other children soon knock a kid into shape if he does not abide by the rules they have accepted for a game. It helps for parents to show the way and accustom a child to these ideas before school begins. Once there, the child will be under pressure to conform to the rules of that society, and the rules of the playground seem inviolate. A system of rules develops and all players must voluntarily accept them if they join in or the game is wrecked. A preparation for life perhaps?

setting up games

If you are to set up games for groups of children, get to **know the rules and details of the game beforehand**. Be absolutely firm and fair in all dealings.

Take into account the various talents and weaknesses of the children who are to play. Choose games which are appropriate and do not play on the weaknesses of one child or show him or her up in a bad light. If you have to join in too, remember to submit to all rules as though you were a child – no special treatment for adults in games! Help younger or less able kids to keep up by giving them carefully assigned parts to play. If a child does not want to join in a group game, let him or her sit it out and help you judge it. A reluctant player can keep score or time keep. Never draw attention to this or embarrass the child, but give a task within this child's ability range and encourage him or her to cope with it.

Before beginning a new game with a group, run through it a couple of times so that everyone can be sure to understand it before they do it for real.

Passions for board games develop as a child learns to cope with losing at chutes and ladders. Logical strategic games such as Chinese Checkers can be started as young as four or five, and this usually becomes chess quite soon. By nine years old the dreaded monotony of Monopoly has them in its grip, and they go on to play more inventive board games every year.

games and cooped-up groups

Games will be useful for groups when you have:

rainyday moods

There are days when a group of children sits cooped-up indoors. Not bored exactly, but with that restlessness that parents soon recognise as 'rainyday behaviour'. They may need some structured games for a while.

indoor parties

There are birthday parties in mid-winter when you and your living room are swamped with twelve large, boisterous party guests. Family occasions can also assemble quite a group of kids together and games can make a great success of that boring patch after lunch.

visitors

If you have two kids, it only needs one friend each, or two visiting cousins, for you to have double the number of vigorous bodies contained in the same space.

strangers

There are times when several children are thrown together; ages may vary greatly and they may not know each other. You and a game could be the catalyst that brings them together.

Here are games to play in cooped-up situations, mostly one room, with a few kids. These can be adjusted and used for two players or expanded into teamwork for several. There are ideas in other sections of this book that would help you in this situation: look for Matchstick Puzzles, Word Games, Guessing Games, Dressing up Box, Stories, and Sound and Rhythm.

• • • • •

sardines   Age 4 and up

Preparation: None.

A popular oldie, yet to each new generation of children it seems fresh. One child hides in a suitable place and all the other players hunt for this sardine. When they find him, they silently squeeze in beside him. Eventually the whole group becomes one giggling mass of arms and legs, under a bed or in a cupboard.

musical statues, bumps, chairs, and islands   Age 4 and up

Preparation: Music and record player or tape recorder, chairs, pieces of newspaper.

All these musical games are basically the same idea and known to everyone who has ever played a game at a children's party. I list them here simply to remind you of the variations.

All players dance and move about to disco music. When the music stops they stand absolutely still as **Statues**. Anyone who moves is out.

In the **Bumps** version, they sit down on the floor with a bump as the music stops, the last to sit down is out.

In **Musical Chairs** there is a row of chairs, but one fewer than the number of children present. When the music stops they must sit on a chair quickly. The person left standing is out. Remove one chair each round.

Islands are pieces of newspaper placed at random all over the floor. When the music stops players dash to islands and must have their feet fully on the paper. Anyone not on paper is out, even if one foot is on. Remove some sheets each round until you have the last few stalwarts landing huddled together on one tiny fragment of paper.

pin the tail on the donkey
Age 4 and up

Preparation: Picture, something to be attached, tack, blindfold.

Played by every four-year-old at some stage there are many variations to this game and it can be kept alive as children get older by tailoring it to the occasion. The basic idea – of drawing a picture and blindfolding a player who must then attach something to that picture in the right place – can be adapted to any theme. The picture does not have to be a donkey, it could be an animal on which you 'pin' whiskers, a huge punk head on which you 'pin' an earring, or a pirate on which you 'pin' a black eye patch. Clown parties can use this game with a pom pom to be stuck on top of the clown's hat. Hallowe'en witches could have teeth stuck on. Tie on a blindfold securely, then turn the child around twice. Now let him try to 'pin the tail on the donkey'.

• • • • •

flying feather
Age 5 and up

Preparation: Check that no player is allergic to feathers. Pull a feather from a pillow.

Sit in a circle and, by puffing and blowing, keep the feather in the air. If it falls and touches a child, he or she is out.

• • • • •

hunt the thimble
Age 5 and up

Preparation: Send all the players out of the room and hide the thimble where it can be seen without moving the objects or furniture.

Call everyone in to look for the thimble. This game requires a fair amount of self control for young players not to shout out when they see the missing thimble. As a player sees it, he or she must simply sit down quietly.

Mr. Grump
Age 5 and up

Preparation: Place several wrapped sweets inside two thick brown paper bags and tie closed. Draw Mr. Grump's horrible ugly face on the outside bag. Suspend Mr. Grump from a doorway or overhead beam. One wooden spoon.

This game serves as a safe release for any aggressive feelings harboured in the heart of even the most angelic child.

Explain to the children that Mr. Grump hates kids, never gives them any sweets, is mean and nasty and keeps them all for himself. Give each child in turn the wooden spoon and a chance to bash old Grump with it. The others stand well away. Eventually the bag breaks and the sweets fall out. Although this game may sound tame on paper, it has been hilariously played year after year in our house with the character of Mr. Grump being defamed further each time. Some children remember him from the previous year and even when I think they have outgrown it, ask, 'Is Mr. Grump coming this time?'

speed threading
Age 5 and up

Preparation: Prepare nylon fishing line and items to be threaded: beads, macaroni bits, drinking straws cut up, buttons, odd nuts and bolts, etc from the tool box.

The object of the game is to thread these items on to the line at speed. The team or person finishing first wins. The easiest way of managing this as a team game is to have each player thread one of each item you have collected, so they thread on one bead, one piece of macaroni and one button, etc, and pass the line to the next team mate, who threads on the next round of items.

• • • • •

dead lions
Age 5 and up

Preparation: None.

This is the game you announce when the noise and chaos of the last few games has reached a peak and you want to calm things down a bit.

All the players lie as still as possible on the floor while the game leader goes around trying to make someone move or giggle by talking and making various rude and funny remarks. No touching is allowed but untruths are permitted such as 'There is this enormous worm crawling up your leg!' Anyone who moves or giggles must help the leader try to make others move. Tiny sounds, snuffles, snorts and stifled giggles count as moves.

snake hiss
Age 6 and up

Preparation: None.

All players take a deep breath and let the air out slowly in a 'sss' sound. This is a contest to see whose breath lasts longest. Most people improve their technique after a little practice so it's wise to have a trial run first.

• • • • •

coin towers
Age 6 and up

Preparation: A large quantity of pennies.

The object is to see who can build the highest tower of coins without the lot coming tumbling down. If played in teams, you will need enough coins to have each team building at the same time. They must play against the clock and see whose tower is highest in two minutes.

• • • • •

clothes peg relay
Age 6 and up

Preparation: A bundle of clothes pegs.

Divide the players into two teams, and sit them down on the floor in two lines. The first person in each team is given 8 clothes pegs which are placed between the fingers of each hand. The first player turns towards the next and offers his hands with the pegs held between the fingers. The next player must take hold of the pegs between his or her fingers in the same way without dropping any of them, and pass them on to the next in the team. The team that passes the pegs down to the last player in the team first, wins.

suction
Age 6 and up

Preparation: A packet of drinking straws (one for each player) and a packet of small edible items, such as raisins or smarties. Two small bowls per player.

Each player has before him or her a small bowl of raisins or smarties. They must suck one on to the end of the straw and keep it there, then run across the carpet to a second bowl awaiting them at the finish. Raisins or smarties are dropped into the second bowl. The process is repeated until all the raisins or smarties are in the second bowl.

Teams may play this as a relay, when one player has dropped the raisin he or she returns to the start and the next team mate starts off.

NB For safety, always use raisins or smarties that are too large ever to get into and up a drinking straw and choke a child.

• • • • •

ping pong races
Age 7 and up

Preparation: A ping pong ball for each player, and a drinking straw each. A starting and finishing line.

By blowing through a straw, the players race their balls along the course.

There are many variations with this game. If you have the space, an obstacle course can be made through which the balls must pass. Cardboard tubes and a wall of marbles may be part of this construction. The first player to navigate this course without toppling the marbles, is the winner.

If there are several players, they can be divided into two teams and the game is played as a relay race. One player from each team blows the ball along the course, and returns to hand it on to the next. Each player holds a personal straw. Team mates may shriek and cheer on their fellow blowers, but it is not permitted to try to blow back an opponent's ball!

blow soccer
Age 7 and up

Preparation: A table tennis ball and goals made from cardboard boxes, a table.

Set up the goals at either end of the table. Divide the players into two teams. Players now play a form of soccer aiming to get the ball into the opponent's goal. The other team will naturally defend their goal and try in turn to score. If your team blows the ball off the table, the others have first blow, starting from where it went off the table.

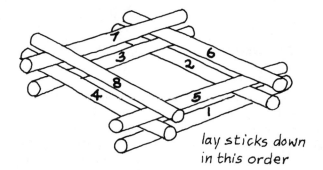

lay sticks down in this order

log cabin skyscraper
Age 7 and up

Preparation: Matches or straws.

Which team or group can build the highest skyscraper using matches or straws laid one on top of another in the time-honoured log cabin manner? The higher the better, but they do tend to fall down! Set a time limit. Count matches if there is a dispute.

• • • • •

phantôme
Age 7 and up

Preparation: A large selection of things from which houses and tents could be built: old curtains, bedspreads, sheets, tablecloths, chairs, etc.

Divide the children into two teams. Send one team out of the room. The remaining team constructs a 'den' which should be covered on all sides so that you cannot see inside it easily. A certain number of the members of this team are hidden inside the den; the others hide elsewhere in the room. Bring in the other team, who must guess by looking closely at the wonderful structure and any visible human limbs how many players are hidden inside it. They can walk round it, look at it from all sides, but may not touch. Swop over and let the other team have a go.

•••••

dummies
Age 7 and up

Preparation: None.

This is played in groups of four. One person is chosen for the dummy. The other three carry the dummy into a 'weird' place (in the words of one enthusiastic player), and proceed to position him. The dummy can't speak or move out of position, but must stay as arranged. The first dummy to move or laugh is out.

egg flip
Age 7 and up

Preparation: Tiddley-winks and empty egg cartons.

Divide the players into two teams. Set the eggboxes at a distance and mark a starting line at the opposite end of the room. Divide tiddley-winks equally amongst players. One member of each team stands ready at the start; the others, in an agreed order, await their turns.

On the signal to begin, the two team members race their tiddley-winks across the floor towards, and hopefully into, the eggboxes. As soon as a player gets a tiddley-wink into one of the hollows of the eggbox, the next player from this team sets out. The first team to complete wins. (Move the tiddley-winks in the traditional way by flipping them forward by pressing on one edge with another tiddley-wink. On a carpet they jump quite high into the air!)

•••••

magnetic fishing
Age 7 and up

Preparation: Pieces of paper torn into small fragments, paper clips, small magnets, pieces of string, little rods or sticks (optional). On each piece of paper write a forfeit or an IOU for a reward. Attach a paperclip to each of these. Attach a magnet to each piece of string (or rod and line). To create the illusion of a fishpond, use an old deep carton or a playpen. If you have neither, simply group a few chairs together and put the pieces of paper with their messages and paperclips into the circle on the floor formed by the chairs.

The players fish with their rods or lines, they pull up catches and read their messages. Rewards may be small sweets, fruit or party favours; forfeits should be performed at the end and should be amusing and entertaining for everyone. See p. 115 for a few ideas for forfeits.

apple bobbing
Age 7 and up

Preparation: A bucket of water and some apples.

This old favourite scarcely needs describing, so this is simply a reminder of the fun to be had as players try to get a grip on the floating apples with their teeth – hands behind their backs. Apples are eaten when retrieved.

• • • • •

dangling doughnuts
Age 7 and up

Preparation: Set up a 'washing line' of string slung across a room, or outside. From this line, suspend doughnuts, each on a piece of string. You should end up with a line of dangling doughnuts, each a little distance apart.

Players hold their hands behind their backs and try to eat the doughnuts off the strings as they swing and sway. Other players who are waiting their turn may call out and try to put them off by making them laugh.

• • • • •

forehead squeeze
Age 7 and up

Preparation: A number of tennis balls or oranges. Divide players into two teams.

The object is for two players in each team to carry a ball or orange from one end of the room to the other and back again by holding it between their foreheads. If dropped, start again. When the first pair completes their circuit, the next pair in that team begin. Hand over the orange quickly. There is quite an art in moving in tandem with your partner and gently covering the distance while hurrying.

snow or flour mountain
Age 8 and up

Preparation: A mountain of flour with a cherry on the top. Plastic sheeting on the floor. A spoon.

Another party classic! Give each child a turn to remove a spoonful of flour to another bowl without making the cherry fall. If the cherry falls, the player must try to eat it off the mountain without using their hands. Replace the mountain and add a new cherry as needed.

• • • • •

egyptian mummies
Age 8 and up

Preparation: A vast quantity of cheap toilet paper rolls

This is a wonderful party game and a true ice-breaker. Divide the players into pairs. One is to be the mummy; the other is to wrap the mummy in endless layers of toilet paper, wound round from head to toe. Leave slits for eyes and breating. Round and round they will twist, some running round the mummy, others getting the mummy to turn until giddiness takes over. It is not easy to encase your partner totally from head to toe. (A moment for the camera!) The first pair to complete wins. The fun of this is more in the playing than the winning.

The paper is used later for clearing up spills from the party, wiping hands and general cleaning.

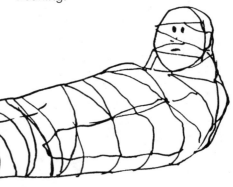

mad hatters
Age 8 and up

Preparation: Newspapers and sellotape.

Each player must fashion the craziest hat ever from newspaper within a time limit. Give out plenty of newspaper to each person along with a roll of tape. Set the timer, and have each player model his or her creation after the time is up.

• • • • •

chocolate carving
Age 8 and up

Preparation: Rubber gloves, knife and fork, wooden board, pair of dice, thick large slab of chocolate, some dressing up clothes: wig, hat, scarf, funny shoes and skirt or trousers. Plastic sheet.

The players sit around in a circle. Put the chocolate on the board in the middle with a plastic sheet beneath. On the floor next to this lay the knife and fork and the clothes and gloves.

Have the players throw the dice in turn until someone gets a double six. As fast as possible this player rushes to put on all the clothes, shoes and rubber gloves and then tries to carve and eat a square of chocolate. Meanwhile the players continue taking turns to throw the dice. As soon as someone throws another double six, that player has quickly to change places with the person attacking the chocolate. Clothes must come off one and be put on by the other . . . really fast. Players are often just about to place the chocolate in their mouths when the next double six is called.

Dressing and undressing at speed with funny clothes and rubber gloves, clumsy and awkward efforts to cut the chocolate and the pressure of the dice throwing add to the general atmosphere. Everyone laughs so much that they can hardly cope with all that they have to do.

limbo dancing
Age 9 and up

Preparation: One broom handle supported on chairs or held by players. Disco music. This can be played indoors or out.

Initially the handle is held shoulder high by players, as one by one the others dance and shimmy beneath it without touching it or the floor. They bend backwards from the knees and hips, shuffling forward. After each round, the handle is lowered and the dancers still in the game attempt to pass under it once more. Eventually it is a few inches from the ground and supple contortions and meagre measurements are needed to get through. Anyone touching the handle or the floor is out. Finally there are one or two players fighting or wriggling it out.

touch and guess
Age 9 and up

Preparation: Place various objects – such as a comb, a pair of blunt nosed scissors, a rubber, a teaspoon, a pencil, and other small items – into a thick woolly sock or a pair of wool tights. Give each child a pencil and a piece of paper.

The players are each allowed a set time in which to feel the contents of the sock through the thick wool and guess what is in there. Each writes these guesses down. At the end compare all lists and see whose is the most accurate. This game can be made easier or more difficult depending on the selection of items you use.

burglar spotting

Age 8–10

Preparation: A set of 'burglar's clothes', paper and pencils. This burglar disguise is for one child only and could include a moustache, wig, hat, raincoat, balaclava (or an old sock cut for eye and nose), ballpoint tattoo or eyebrow pencil freckles, shoes that the child was not wearing on arrival at the party, trousers, plus a bag for the loot.

Tell the players that you are from the local police station and that you are investigating a robbery. A suspicious looking character was seen escaping, and running this way. Tell them to be on the look-out for anyone suspicious. A little later, unobtrusively take one player out of the room while the others are occupied. Dress this player in the disguise and add the bag in which to haul off the loot. Make certain that the burglar is unrecognisable as the child who came to the party.

Come back into the room and ask if anyone has seen the burglar. He has been spotted nearby. As pre-arranged with the burglar, shout 'POLICE'. At this signal the burglar runs swiftly past the window, or through the room, but not close enough to be caught. Now ask those who saw him to write down a detailed description of him. Can anyone do an identikit drawing?

If the players are seated, it may be possible for the burglar to run once around the room before vanishing. The most accurate description wins.

• • • • •

read and search

Age adaptable

Preparation: First assemble all the items you will be hiding. You need more than one of each per player, because a few are never found, and the odd person takes two of something by mistake. Before you hide them (and forget where they are), list them and draw up the clues. Paper bags.

The outline of this game is very simple; it is how you do it that makes it imaginative and exciting.

The game is played by giving each person a list of clues – cryptic and clever for older players, direct and easy if they are young. They roam the house looking for items like a great big treasure hunt, and they must return to you with all the items in a paper bag to be checked against your list.

If the game is to be played by little people, a straightforward list will be all they can handle if reading is still new to them. Your clues might say:

> a piece of wool
> a coin
> a match
> a piece of blue ribbon
> an elastic band
> a cork
> a bottle top
> a piece of string
> a piece of newspaper
> a spool of thread
> a tiny silverfoil wrapped chocolate
> a tweed/silk scrap

For the older age group, nine year olds for example, you could branch out a bit. The piece of wool could be described as 'something from sheep', the coin as 'something with Abraham Lincoln's head on it', etc. Simple, but needing a moment's thought.

As the players get older you will need more cryptic clues, rather like crossword clues. Some clues might indicate the place to look . . .

'My initials are the same as a famous war time leader's' *(FR)*

'So far and no further . . .' *(sofa)*

'Alexander Bell wouldn't recognise me now' *(new shape telephone)*

'Italian word for softly' *(piano)*

'To head a committee' *(chair)*

A lemon might be described as 'A fruit that reminds you of a French car.' *(Citron=Citroen, etc.)*

I bet you can't . . .

A series of challenges for two or more players. Some would make ideal forfeits in games such as Magnetic Fishing, see page 111.

- Throw rings from preserving jars on to up-turned chair legs.

- Roll a marble on to a target (a pyramid of marbles set at a distance).

- Drop a penny into a milk bottle from a height. To do this, children stand up and drop from eyelevel to a bottle which is on the floor between their feet.

- Bounce a ping pong ball along a table and into an egg carton, or blow this ball along the table and into an egg carton attached to the under edge of the table with tape.

- Drop a coin into a glass submerged in a bucket of water.

- Hit a target with a paper aeroplane from across a room.

- Tell without looking at a watch when one minute is up.

- Write down the alphabet backwards in under one minute.

- Stand on your head and balance your knees on your elbows.

- Peel an apple in one continuous spiral without once breaking the peel. Don't peel thickly!

- Draw a picture of an elephant while blindfolded.

- Taste the difference between a slice of apple and a slice of potato while blindfolded and holding your nose tightly.

- Touch the tip of your nose with your tongue.

- Estimate the speed the car is travelling at without seeing the speedometer.

- Turn round (blindfolded) three times and then say which way you are facing.

- Say one of the following fast six times without a mistake:

  Any noise annoys an oyster, but
  A noisy noise annoys an oyster most.

  Red lorry, yellow lorry

  Betty Botter bought some butter,
  'But,' she said 'This butter's bitter,
  If I put it in my batter,
  It will make my batter bitter.
  But a bit of better butter
  Would make my batter better.'
  So she bought a bit of butter
  Better than her bitter butter
  And she put it in her batter
  And it made her batter better.
  So twas better Betty Botter bought a bit of
      better butter!

  Swim Sam swim,
  Swim like a snow white swan swims.
  You know how to swan swim.
  Six sharp shivering sharks
  Are about to snap your limbs.
  So smite them swiftly as you swim,
  Swim Sam swim.
                                    Tracey Kenyon

When looking for more 'I bet you can't' challenges don't forget Matchstick Puzzles (page 37), Paradoxes (page 35), favourite riddles, Coin Puzzle (page 36) and completing slogans.

in the
sickroom

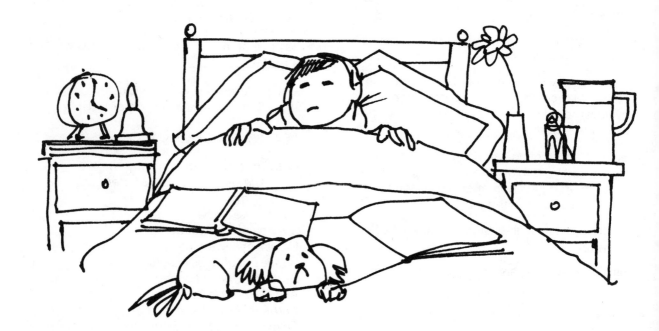

There is no slick checklist of ideas that can transform the situation for a sick listless child. Also, each illness is different. One child might not feel up to much, and another may be feeling all right but be quarantined for a while. The ideas grouped here may remind you of some aspect of your child's well-being that you *are* able to improve however, and I hope that other parts of this book may prove helpful. Take a look through **In a creative mood** and **Games without toys**, and don't forget story tapes and music.

Unless a child is so ill that bedrest is essential, most kids spend part of the day up and about, or lying on the living room couch during common childhood illnesses. Boredom is a problem, but you will generally find an unwell child will prefer to do something more suited to a younger age than his present level. Concentration spans are short, yet capturing someone's interest takes minds off the illness for a while.

Sure signs of improvement are when mischief returns, and kids get better with a bang! In the meanwhile I hope these pages can be of help.

comfort

sympathy

Your young patient will need all the sympathy you can manage. This is the amazing cure for hurts and misery of all kinds. Busy parents coping with the extra work an illness brings may forget to make time for giving sympathy. Make a fuss of your patient and you will notice an improvement in mood.

••••

surprises

Break the routine with little surprises: a flower on a tray of lunch, a wash with special scented water, a change of bed linen, or even changing the position of the bed. These seemingly small things loom large in the life of a sickly child.

•••••

cheer up!

Your child will often be frustrated and weepy if very young. Activities normally loved and found easy might seem too difficult. Little jokes, like cartoon drawings on a paper placemat, will leave a good memory, and specially folded paper napkins are quick to prepare and will entertain.

flashlight

A flashlight might give the child comfort in the night and something interesting to play with beneath bedclothes during the day. Remember how your skin glowed red when you put your hand over a flashlight?

•••••

body comfort

Does this child need extra pillows? A different lightweight cover over the bed? If, like most kids, yours will not stay in bed unless too ill to get up, put socks on feet so that each time they are out of the bed they at least stay warm. If the child is sitting up and playing, a soft top, sweatshirt or tracksuit top will be snug and comfortable to wear. Avoid sweaters that are too tight under the arms.

folded napkins:

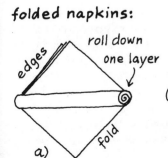

a) edges — roll down one layer — fold

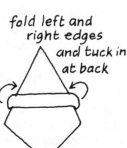

fold left and right edges and tuck in at back

tuck cutlery into pocket

b) open out napkin and fold in half diagonally; roll up from base of triangle; fold spiralled tube in half and plunge into glass

light

Does the overhead light shine too brightly into the patient's eyes? The eyes may be sensitive to light and the normal light on the ceiling may seem overpowering. A soft nightlight can be reassuring.

• • • • •

where?

In a home where bedrooms may be on another floor, can you move your patient to a room on the kitchen level, or save yourself trips upstairs any other way? If not too ill, let a child be with the family in the kitchen or living room rather than alone upstairs.

If you can have the bed on wheels – well worth doing if the illness is a long one – then the position of the bed can be more easily changed and the child could be brought to another room or have his or her view altered. Alternatively, do you have somewhere else this child can lie down? A day bed or sunlounger, perhaps, to let the patient be with the family (if not madly infectious). There are many lightweight fold-up beds or sofa beds, and you might find this breaks the routine.

• • • • •

pot pourri

The air in the room can be sweetened with a pot pourri mixture and the patient might enjoy making new ones, see page 60.

• • • • •

bed table

An up-turned carton with holes cut in the sides for the knees will make a good, light and comfy bed table.

time

The days stretch on unendingly for a child confined to bed. Many young children find the thought of a week frighteningly long at the best of times, and the prospect of a long stay in bed, in the same room, can seem daunting to the whole family.

It helps to tackle the subject of time very directly. A calendar can be used to mark off the days as they pass. Mark when friends are coming to visit, or favourite TV programmes will be shown.

Small events can be used to break up periods of time, which can be marked by using an alarm clock. A young child may be fascinated by the magic of this device and feel proud to be entrusted with it. The child may be left to read or play for half an hour while a parent is elsewhere in the home. The alarm can be set reassuringly for 30 minutes, and the child can be sure of knowing that when the half hour is up the parent will visit again. In this way, you might get a couple of things done, and your child will not feel too abandoned. Small children quickly master the setting of these limits and can operate alarm clocks at a very young age even if they cannot tell the time! Modern digital clocks are the easiest.

communication
··

How will the patient call you if he or she needs to? A small hand bell may be the answer, but each child has a solution to this, including whistles, tooters and various weird noises. Most fun are the contraptions rigged up with pieces of string looped through a curtain ring or over a convenient hook, with a noise-making object at the other end. A wooden spoon organised to hit the metal lid of a cake tin each time the string is yanked will make an effective gong. These make calling you a moment of hilarity rather than a whine.

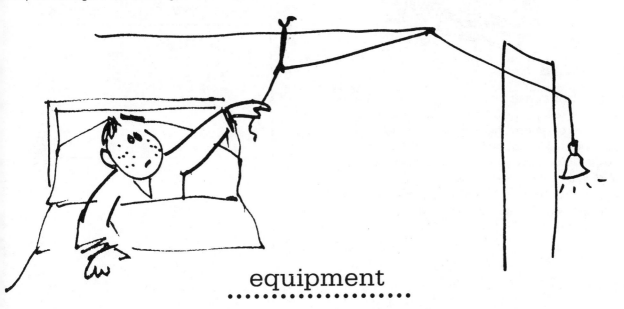

equipment
··

It helps to make a few adaptations to the room.

bed table

A large piece of board laid over two chairs can form a large convenient bed table, a good surface on which to play and eat meals. The board could go under the bed when not in use.

A large tray or, better still, a cut-down box is a good surface for puzzles and games as the rim prevents the pieces from flying all over the bed. If cutting down a carton for this, cut one long edge lower than the other edges and face this towards the patient for easier access.

storage

Haberdashery departments sell multipocket shoe storage bags. These are helpful as organisers near the child. They hang from a coat hanger and items needed regularly can be packed into the pockets and easily retrieved.

Place crayons in a jam jar so that the colours may be easily seen through the glass and they are kept together, rather than rolling all over the bed.

easel

A cardboard easel is easy to make. It folds away, is lightweight on the bed and costs nothing. Use a large piece of corrugated cardboard. This will be ideal for drawing and painting projects and can be a help to someone ill in bed and needing a light-weight surface to write or draw against.

clipboard

A clipboard is a great aid to writing and drawing as the paper will be held still and there is a rigid surface to press on. This clipboard can be turned into a book holder, giving the arms a rest. Have the child lie down with knees bent and lean the clipboard against the raised knees. Hang a wire coat hanger from the top of the clipboard and bend its 'shoulders' around the open book, and the lower edge up to form a ledge.

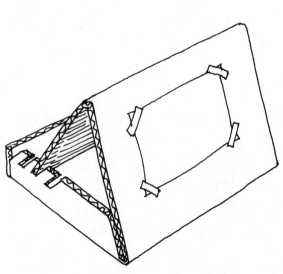

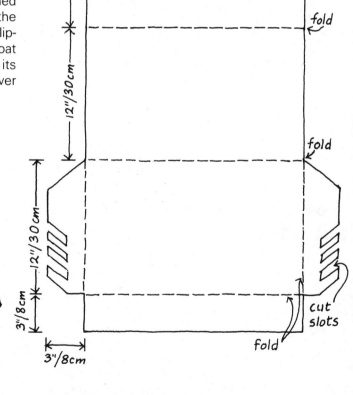

something to look at

Staring for hours at the same four walls is utterly depressing. Create movement and interest with goldfish in a bowl, a hamster or guineapig (if the child is not allergic), a fast growing plant, or bird feeders outside the window. These provide effortless entertainment for the child.

Mobiles and windchimes are peaceful to watch and listen to. These are easily made and easily bought. There is a simple chime made from milk bottle tops on page 99.

something to do

On-going, long-term projects that have the advantage of only demanding small spurts of energy will sustain interest for a convalescing child. Short projects are rewarding then and there. A good combination of both is needed to keep a balance.

• • • •

grow a mini garden

A miniature landscape in a container allows a child to picture scenes and make them real. See page 59.

• • • •

wool

Teach the patient to knot, knit or crochet. With chunky wool a quick result is achieved even if only a small amount is done each day. Simple braiding produces beautiful bookmarks.

jigsaw

Work on major jigsaws if the child is old enough. Use a large kitchen tea tray to work on so pieces won't fall off the edges. It can be placed on a bed, or on a table and then quickly removed. A cut down cardboard carton with shallow sides is a good base too.

• • • • •

music

Favourite music can be soothing or stimulating. Tapes are more controllable than radio, and the child can make a list of choices which can be played again and again.

Some enterprising teenage brothers recorded their little sister's favourite singles on to one tape when she broke her leg; this gave hours of pleasure. Do you have a member of the family who always fancied himself as a disc jockey?

stories

Stories on tape are available commercially, but so much more fun are stories read by friends or family all doing different voices and special sound effects. When a visitor comes, try to persuade the newcomer to record a story, or part of one, on tape to play to your patient later. The **Fun and fantasy** section contains suggestions on how to use stories in many different ways.

• • • • •

themes

Some illnesses suggest in themselves themes for games, such as the time when all the kids in our building had chickenpox. We thought of every game we could that used or contained spots. Dominoes are obvious. We expanded into tiddley-winks, games with round counters and many more spotted variations, with a couple of dot-to-dots as well. We made a very spotty cake, a quite revolting Jell-O covered in blotches and spots, chocolate chip cookies, and wore clothes with, yes, spots. This did help some kids feel better about their terrible looking skin. It became a joke. As if this were not enough, we drew chickens with millions of spots on paper napkins and paper table cloths. The fun of preparing all this for a shared meal helped them forget their misery and ugliness.

have a meal in a foreign land

This game can transport a bored and cooped-up kid to another country. Pick a country, for example Italy. The meal will consist of pizza or spaghetti Bolognese and perhaps a little cassata or other Italian ice cream. There is fun to be had laying a table or tray. Use the colours red, green and white, discuss the flag and the theme as you do this. There is a fascinating variety of pasta shapes with entertaining names – why not expand your usual choice to embrace some of these? Coloured paper napkins might be red on a white cloth, with something green – candles perhaps?

Do you know of any songs to sing? Records to play? Travel books or posters/calendars to look at? This game can be expanded in many directions. Drawing the map of the country can take up some time and you may know someone who has recently visited this place. With luck you can persuade such travellers to come and tell your child something about the visit. For a child who is confined to the home for a long time with an illness or broken limb, this can go on in stages for a few days. Draw on library books for help.

Children learn foreign languages so easily that a few words taught during a meal can be useful later. If you know how to count, can name a few objects on the table and say 'please' and 'thank you', you are on the way to being a linguist.

If you use China as your country, teach the child to eat with chopsticks.

After doing this more than once, your child will develop a sprinkling of words in another language, a taste for new foods and some vague geography, all in the convivial atmosphere of mealtime.

• • • •

diary

Keeping a diary only takes small amounts of energy from time to time. Your child might record the antics of any pets, the birds seen at the window, any jokes told him that day, or the changing colour of the leaves. A weather record can show how often the weather forecast was right or wrong. Listen to it each day on the radio, and note down how many hours of sunshine there were, or if it poured with rain instead.

• • • •

extras

While having to take it easy your child will enjoy a magic slate or etch-a-sketch set, electronic games, travel sets of chess, Chinese checkers, solitaire, tic-tac-toe and those marvelous crayons that will 'paint' when dipped in water. These last give the child the opportunity to paint without liquid paint sloshing around on the bedclothes.

This is the time to consider finding a penfriend. If your patient is a potential letter-writer there will not be much for you to do. If he or she is not, then pictures, drawings, stamps and photos can be collected and sent to the penfriend. It is all worth it when a letter arrives in the post.

Simple games such as finger puppets and hand games will entertain a very young child and are the work of a moment. See pages 25–26.

Offer your patient a magnifying glass for looking at things with new eyes.

Enjoy a pack of playing cards, magnetic puzzles, even those paper clips on a magnetic pyramid which are standard office equipment these days but fun to mess about with. Another office item we have enjoyed are the sheets of coloured sticky circles. These are used to make mosaic pictures and are easier to deal with than the packets of sticky shapes sold for children's use. Each spot is prised off its backing sheet; they are not loose and therefore not lost. Paper clips and a magnet can be used for fishing over the side of the bed (see page 111).

index

· · · · · · · · · · · ·